Mendelssohn

The Illustrated Lives of the Great Composers.

Mendelssohn

Mozelle Moshansky.

Omnibus Press

London/New York/Sydney

Cover design and art direction by Pearce Marchbank.
Cover photography by George Taylor, Rembrandt Bros.
Cover styled by Annie Hanson.

Printed in Great Britain by BPC Wheatons Ltd, Exeter

© Mozelle Moshansky 1982
First published by Midas Books in 1982.
This edition published in 1984 by Omnibus Press, a division of Book Sales Limited.

Order No. OP 42381
UK ISBN 0.7119.0252.6
US ISBN 0.89524.207.9

Exclusive Distributors:
Book Sales Limited,
8/9 Frith Street,
London W1V 5TZ
England

120 Rothschild Avenue,
Rosebery,
Sydney,
NSW 2018
Australia.

Music Sales Corporation,
257 Park Avenue South,
New York, NY 10010, U.S.A.

To the Music Trade Only:
Music Sales Limited,
8/9 Frith Street,
London W1V 5TZ,
England.

Contents

Acknowledgements

My father, friends and colleagues were of great encouragement during the preparation of this book. Dick and Katrina Burnett, Ruth Hewlett, Christine Hogg, Robert Maycock, Simon Mundy, Ateş and Josephine Orga, and Nigel Simeone all took an interest, for which I am grateful. I must extend thanks also to my publishers, Ian and Kathleen Morley-Clarke, and to my editor, Robert F. Hardcastle.

Also to the British Museum, the Bodleian Library, Oxford, Mary Evans Picture Library, Radio Times Hulton Picture Library, the Mansell Collection and George Rainbird Limited for permission to reproduce illustrations.

Select Bibliography

Benedict, Julius *A Sketch of the Life and Works of the late Felix Mendelssohn-Bartholdy* (London, 1850)

Blunt, Wilfred *On Wings of Song* (London, 1974)

Crum, Margaret *Felix Mendelssohn-Bartholdy* (Oxford, 1972)

Devrient, Eduard *My Recollections of Felix Mendelssohn-Bartholdy;* translated by Natalia Macfarren (London, 1869)

Grove's Dictionary of Music and Musicians. Article by Sir George Grove (London, 1878). 5th edition, article by Percy M. Young (London, 1954)

Hensel, Sebastian *The Mendelssohn Family;* translated by Karl Klingemann (2 vols., London, 1880)

Hiller, Ferdinand *Mendelssohn, Letters and Recollections;* translated by M.E. von Glehn (London, 1874)

Horsley, Sophy and Fanny *Mendelssohn and his Friends in Kensington;* edited by Rosamund Brunel Gotch (London, 1934)

Horton, John *Mendelssohn's Chamber Music* (London, 1972)

Jacob, H.E. *Felix Mendelssohn and His Times;* translated by Richard and Clara Winston (London, 1963)

Jenkins, David and Mark Visocchi *Mendelssohn in Scotland* (London, 1978)

Kupferberg, Herbert *Felix Mendelssohn, His Life, His Family, His Music* (New York, 1972)

Lampadius, W.A. *Life of Felix Mendelssohn-Bartholdy;* translated by M.E. von Glehn (London, 1876)

Marek, George R. *Gentle Genius, The Life of Felix Mendelssohn* (New York, 1972)

Mendelssohn-Bartholdy, Felix *Letters;* translated by Gisela Seldon-Goth (New York, 1945)

Petitpierre, Jacques *The Romance of the Mendelssohns* (New York, 1947)

Polko, Elise *Reminiscences of Felix Mendelssohn-Bartholdy;* translated by Lady Wallace (London, 1869)

Radcliffe, Philip *Mendelssohn* (London, 1954; revised 1976)

Rockstro, William Smyth *Mendelssohn* (London, 1883)

Scholes, Percy A. *The Oxford Companion to Music* (London, 1938)

Stratton, Stephen S. *Mendelssohn* (London, 1901)

Werner, Eric *Mendelssohn;* translated by Dika Newlin (New York, 1963)

Werner, Jack *Mendelssohn's Elijah* (London, 1965)

Chapter 1

Beginnings

'They are an ancient people, a famous people, an enduring people, and a people who in the end have generally attained their objects. I cannot help remembering that the Jews have outlived Assyrian Kings, Egyptian Pharaohs, Roman Caesars and Arabian Caliphs' — DISRAELI

When, on 4 November, 1847, worn out by care and overwork, Felix Mendelssohn died, the world of music was stunned.

At thirty-eight, Germany's prince of music, this 'modest and simple man', one of the century's brightest and most attractive stars, was no more.

In Leipzig, where he died, a city mourned. 'An awful stillness prevails', wrote an English student at the Conservatory, 'we feel as if the King were dead'. Three days later, the Paulinckirche, draped in black, saw the first of many services to be held throughout Germany. The Berlin *Staatszeitung* reported:

Mendelssohn's body was brought to church, preceded by a band of wind instruments playing Beethoven's *Funeral March;* the pallbearers were Moscheles, David, Hauptmann and Gade:*

The professors of the Conservatory, with Mendelssohn's brother as chief mourner, and several guilds and societies from Leipzig and Dresden, followed the coffin. After the pastor's funeral oration, an organ prelude and chorales from *St. Paul* and Bach's *St. Matthew Passion* were played by the orchestra under Gade's and David's direction. During the service, the coffin remained open, and the painters Bendemann, Hübner and Richard made drawings of the great man with the wealth of laurel upon his brow.

At eight the same evening, a torchlit procession upwards of a thousand people bore the coffin to the railway station for its journey to Berlin. At ten, the train left, halting at Köthen, Dessau and Halle, being met at each stop by men and women come to pay tribute to the foremost German musician of the day. At seven the next morning, the Prussian capital came into view:

There the coffin, adorned by ivy leaves and a large wreath of laurel, was carried on a hearse drawn by six horses draped in black to the cemetery of Holy Trinity Church. Thousands followed the bier, and Beethoven's *Funeral March* was again played. Clergymen and other friends of the deceased pronounced orations at the grave, and a choir of six hundred sang a hymn by Gröber, *Christ the Resurrection.*

Felix Mendelssohn. After the oil painting by William von Schadow, 1835.

* Schumann and Julius Reitz were also there.

9

'It is impossible to describe the mournful scene', the *Staatszeitung* concluded, 'the men threw earth, and the women and children flowers, on the coffin when it was finally lowered into the grave. Mendelssohn sleeps near that beloved sister whose death so fatally affected him'.

To Karl Klingemann, Felix's brother, Paul, wrote, 'By Fanny's death, our family was shattered *(zerstört);* by Felix's, it is annihilated *(vernichtet).*

As a mark of respect, a concert scheduled at the Leipzig *Gewandhaus* (where Mendelssohn had been music director) was cancelled. But on 14 November, the Viennese première of *Elijah* went ahead, the music stands draped in black, the singers dressed in black. With full Viennese pomp, there lay on the conductor's desk a score and laurel wreath. But no one stood there. The performance was instead directed from a lower dais by the chorus master.

Across the channel, England's grief was no less sharp. Preoccupied with the Irish famine and the violence stemming from it, Queen Victoria still found time with Prince Albert to send to Mendelssohn's widow, Cécile, a more than usually heartfelt message. An even keener appreciation of the Queen's distress is to be found in her diary:

We were horrified, astounded and distressed to read in the papers of the death of Mendelssohn, the greatest musical genius since Mozart, & the most amiable man. He was quite worshipped by those who knew him intimately, & we have so much appreciated and admired his wonderfully beautiful compositions. We liked & esteemed the excellent man & looked up to & revered the wonderful genius, & the great mind, which I fear were too much for the frail delicate body. With it all he was so modest and simple. To feel when one is playing his beautiful music, that he is no more...

Moses Mendelssohn. Felix's grandfather, philosopher and champion of Jewish emancipation.

Of Mendelssohn's superlative gifts, there can be no doubt. At nine, he showed himself a pianist of altogether unusual accomplishment. At ten, he was a precociously talented composer, at sixteen one of genius.

Concurrently, he developed talents that ranged over a multitude of disciplines. Playing violin and organ, sketching with ink or charcoal, painting with watercolours, all this and more he mastered without effort.

A sharp-eyed correspondent, he was at twelve a letter-writer of insight and energy (he once wrote twenty-seven letters, long detailed letters, in a single day). Books he read continuously and came back for more. At twenty-one, two undisputed masterpieces behind him, he was in the forefront of the Bach revival, conducting the first performance in a century of the *St. Matthew Passion*.

As a traveller he was indefatigable, climbing mountains, traversing valleys and fording streams. Soon the most sought after musician of the age, he was eulogised wherever he went. Handsome, charming and urbane, he became a celebrity among celebrities. People everywhere capitulated to his kindness and sincerity. Women adored him. Men admired him.

Felix Mendelssohn was, moreover, rich; after his father's death hugely so. Son of a wealthy banker, he was born to greater comfort and good fortune than any other composer. From the start, all the good things in life were poured out for him. Clothes, music paper, writing materials, all were of the finest. If Abraham and Lea Mendelssohn expected much from their children, their material well-being was assured.

As a result, it is easy to forget that it had not always been so. The Mendelssohn's riches were all newly acquired. Felix's grandfather Moses, 'the son of Mendel' from the small town of Dessau on the banks of the Elbe, came from very different circumstances. Only with difficulty, hunchbacked and undernourished as he was, had he survived a childhood of poverty and deprivation. So determined was he to make a better life, that at fourteen he left home to tramp the eighty or so dusty miles to Berlin, capital of Imperial Prussia, there to seek fame and fortune.

As he approached the city, he would have made for the Rosenthaler Gate. This he would have done because he was a Jew, and the Rosenthaler the only gate by which a Jew might enter the city. It is said that when the guard came to record the day's events, he wrote:

Today there passed through Rosenthaler Gate, six oxen, seven pigs, one Jew.

Apocryphal or not, it hardly matters. At the time, life for Jews all over Europe was hard. In the various German states, they enjoyed few legal rights, living instead under a battery of laws and edicts designed especially to humiliate them.

Rosenthaler Gate

There were restrictions on where a Jew might live and what kind of work he might do. Debarred from all but a few professions, most were compelled to become peddlars, hawking their wares from door to door, or beggars. A Jew could not manufacture goods, nor supply any army or government department. He could not sell food, except to another Jew. He could not own land. A Jewish artist could not

11

become a court portrait painter. If he had musical ability, he was forbidden to teach in any school, save those for Jews. If he needed clothes, he could buy them only at stipulated hours, and had no redress for faulty goods.

Taxes of various kinds were heaped upon him. *Leibzoll,* or 'body tax', extorted from Jewish travellers protection money to ensure their 'safety' on the road. Another *Kalendergeld,* levied a charge for using the Hebrew rather than the Gregorian calendar. In Austria, a 'light tax' was imposed for the lighting of candles on the Sabbath and Holy Days. How this was collected remains a mystery.

In Prussia, ruled by the gifted but irascible Frederick the Great, every Jew was compelled to celebrate his marriage (for which a permit was needed) by purchasing from the royal china factory in Berlin a set of rejects. As a result, Moses Mendelssohn became, on his wedding day, reluctant owner of twenty china monkeys.

Jews, above all, were condemned to live in ghettoes. Even in so relatively enlightened a province as the Cologne Electorate, ruled by bishops sitting in Bonn, Jews were obliged to live in a tiny, squalid sidestreet (the *Judengasse)* as late as 1770, when Beethoven was born.

In Frankfurt, the young Goethe often visited the Jewish quarter, watching the street life and flirting with the pretty Jewish girls. Colonel John Trumbull, the American artist, gives on the other hand a less rosy picture of the same district. The *Judengasse,* Trumbull records, was:

...a very narrow street or rather lane, impassable for carriages with the houses very lofty, old-fashioned, and filthy, not more than a quarter of a mile long — no cross avenue or alley, and a strong gate at each end, carefully closed and secured at tattoo-beat, after which no one is allowed to go out or enter and whoever is found out of the quarter after this time is secured by the city guard and confined. This quarter is said to contain ten thousand of this miserable people, how such a number can exist in such a narrow space is almost incredible, yet (at one of the entrance gates) I saw them crowded together in filth and wretchedness, calculated to generate disease. And how were they to escape from fire after the only two avenues were closed for the night?

When popular feeling ran high, even their lives were in danger. Well could a Jew speak of an 'Isaak, may his light continue to shine', or a 'Rebecka, may her life go on'. Survival was hardly assured, the future clouded with uncertainty.

Matters elsewhere were even worse. For anyone luckless enough to be born a Polish or Lithuanian Jew, the only hope of safety lay in flight. Pillage, rape and arson were commonplaces of existence, and each year hundreds braved wolf-infested forests to reach the border. Between 1710 and 1760 at least nine trials on trumped-up charges are recorded in Poland, after which Jews found 'guilty' of murdering Christian children for ritual purposes, were flayed, tortured and executed by being impaled on sharpened stakes. Massacres took place with monotonous regularity, usually after the harvest failed or bands of marauding cossacks with time to kill had nothing better to do than terrorise some *shtetl* dwellers.

In Spain, the Inquisition was still in full swing. Of 868 cases tried between 1721 and 1727, more than eight hundred were for the 'crime' of Judaism. Of those found guilty, seventy-five were burnt at the stake.

In France, the wind blew hot and cold. Enlightened though he may have been in many ways, Voltaire was, by and large, no friend of Jews, having been swindled by one in a transaction in which he himself had not acted with complete honesty. Even so sensitive a soul as Pascal was not averse to echoing Martin Luther, and recommending that the Jews 'be made miserable because they crucified Him'. Fanaticism everywhere was rife. Only across the channel, in England, were Jews left largely unmolested.

Not every Jew was inclined to take things lying down, and the age was peppered with Jews who rose high and, in not a few cases, fell low. There was Joseph Oppenheimer (1692?-1738), who served both the Elector of Mannheim and Karl Alexander, Duke of Würtemberg. For the latter, he devised a plan, drawn from the British model, for a state bank. A member of the Privy Council, he invented taxes, expanded royal monopolies and, less wisely, accepted bribes, splitting the profits, it was said, with the Duke. When Karl Alexander died, Oppenheimer was arrested, charged and convicted. He was subsequently garotted, and his corpse gruesomely displayed to public view in a cage in the town square: Such was the fate of the man known as 'Jud Süss'. Leon Feuchtwanger told his story in the novel *Paver* (1925).

A little later came Veital Ephraim, official banker to Frederick the Great, free-spending King of Prussia. Under Ephraim's guidance, the Prussian Exchequer bought up gold and silver coins from Holland, Hungary, Poland and Russia, melted them down, mixed them with inferior base metals, re-stamped them and sent them back to their various countries of origin, claiming full value. It was forgery — hugely profitable forgery — on a grand scale. Not for nothing did Berliners sing:

> *Outside silver, inside tin,*
> *Outside honesty, inside sham,*
> *Outside Frederick, inside Ephraim.*

Felix Mendelssohn's maternal grandfather rose to become jeweller to the Prussian court. Restless and dissatisfied, another young Jew walked out of a rabbinical seminary in the country, and made his way to Frankfurt. There, he began a series of financial transactions that brought him to the notice of Landgrave Wilhelm of Hesse-Cassel, and led his heirs to a fortune of some £3 billion. His name was Meyer Rothschild.

Similarly, against a background of prejudice and occasional violence, did Moses Mendelssohn somehow contrive to prosper. From the start, living in an attic room, he learned new languages, English, French, Greek and Latin. Fired by a thirst for knowledge and possessed of a keen intellect, the young man from Dessau read deeply in philosophy, European literature, mathematics and Euclidean geometry.

From abject poverty, he rose first to become a house tutor *(Hauslehrer)*, then a bookeeper and finally senior partner in a silk weaving factory owned by Isaak Bernhard. A man of great distinction, mild and good-natured by temperament, he won at the same time a European reputation as a philosopher and thinker. From Berlin to London his books were read, bringing him the admiration and friendship of many leading figures in the Enlightenment. His *Phädon*, a mock-Platonic treatise on the immortality of the soul first published in 1767, was a popular classic in thirty languages, and excited the attention of the great Immanuel Kant, whose own achievement was for a time eclipsed by that of Mendelssohn.

Firmly resisting attempts to convert him to Christianity, Moses also became famous as a champion of Jewish emancipation and religious tolerance. He translated into German certain of the

14

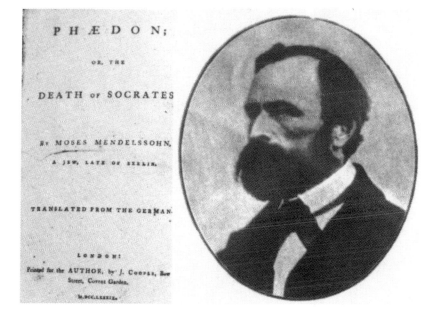

Psalms and the *Pentateuch*. Believing that Judaism was 'revealed legislation' rather than a religion, and that all monotheistic religions were no more than differing interpretations of one truth, 'the German Socrates' as he came to be known, furnished, in *Jerusalem, or of the Religious Force of Judaism* (1783), stylistically his finest achievement, what Kant described as 'irrefutable' proof that the state had no right to interfere in the religion of its citizens. The most sympathetic portrait of Moses had already been penned by his friend, the dramatist Lessing, of whose *Nathan the Wise*, (1775) Mendelssohn is the eloquent, open-handed hero.

Despite his unattractive physique, Moses married happily – his wife was Fromet Guggenheim, daughter of an impecunious Viennese merchant — and in due course became the father of six children. Of three sons, two, Abraham and Joseph, survived infancy to become bankers. The eldest of three daughters, Dorothea was to scandalize her contemporaries by taking as second husband a man much younger than herself — the poet, Friedrich von Schlegel — with whom she had previously philandered for some time.

It was Henriette, however, who was to play the most prominent part in Felix's life. Known by her nieces and nephews as 'Tante Jette', she was for some years headmistress of a school in Paris and, for a time, governess to the daughters of General Sabastiani. Hensel describes her reign in the latter role as 'a brilliant misery', adding, 'What self-sacrifice did Henriette devote to the ungrateful task of making this meagre French soil fruitful by German diligence!'.*
Henriette returned to Berlin in 1824, and was in close touch with her brother Abraham's family until her death seven years later.

*Fanny Sebastiani, an attractive but not especially intelligent child, grew up to marry the son of the Duc de Praslin, by whom, in 1847, she was murdered.

15

Evidently a warm-hearted person, she wrote Felix a letter on his twentieth birthday that opened wistfully, 'My poor Felix; in ten years, no longer a boy!'.

Abraham Mendelssohn, 'formerly the son of my father, now the father of my son' as he was later wryly to describe himself, was born in Berlin in 1776. In 1797, he obtained a junior post in the Paris banking house of Fould and Co. A hard worker he had, by 1803, risen to the position of chief cashier. In Paris, he met Lea Salomon, daughter of the Prussian court jeweller and granddaughter of the banker Daniel Itzig, an educated, musical woman of grace and beauty. Abraham proposed, was accepted, and shortly after his marriage returned to Germany, settling in the Hanseatic free city of Hamburg in partnership with his brother Joseph.

Abraham and Lea suited each other well. Lea could be bright and clever, and a keen student of English, French, Italian and Greek, reading Homer in secret, it is said, lest such a recreation be thought 'unladylike'. Though less gifted than either his father or son, Abraham was nonetheless a man of ability, by nature tough and efficient, and governed by the belief that the gifted man has a duty to strive for perfection and thereby set an example to others. Yet he was capable also of generating love and respect, and between them Abraham and Lea combined attitudes upon which an affectionate and united family could be raised. Abraham, wrote Sebastian Hensel, was 'a harmonious, independent, vigorous character', Lea 'gentle, full of accurate judgement and striking, but never malicious, wit'.

A devoted parent, Abraham's letters to his children indicate his patriarchal solicitude for their well-being:

Your (Felix's) letters have given me pleasure, but in the second I found some traces of carelessness, which I will point out to you when I come home. You must try to speak better, then you will also write better. Your letters, my dear little king of the Moors, also called Paul Hermann, were the best of all, without a single mistake and beautifully short. I praise you for your conduct, of which Mother, Rebecka and Fanny give such a charming account.

And, in the same letter, to Fanny:

You, dear Fanny, have written your first letter very nicely; the second, however, was a little hasty. It does you credit you do not like B's bad jokes; I do not approve them either, and it is wicked to try to make people laugh at what is beautiful and good.

The eldest child, Fanny Cäcilie, was born at the family home, Marten's Mill, on 14 November, 1805; she had, her mother divined, 'Bach fugue fingers'. Next came Jakob Felix Ludwig, on 3 February, 1809. Then, on 11 April, 1811, Rebecka.

Only weeks after the birth of Rebecka, the entire family was forced to flee Hamburg and seek refuge in Berlin. This hasty departure stemmed from the Napoleonic wars ravaging Europe for years past. The reasons are complex, but a few strands stand out. When, in 1806, Bonaparte defeated Prussia on the battlefield, he

16

elected to blockade all trade with England, with whom France was still at war. As a trading port, Hamburg lived by its shipping and its status as an international exchange. It depended for its survival on the continuance of such trade. Merchants were, as a result, faced with a stark alternative. They could obey Bonaparte's orders and see themselves quickly ruined. Or they could become, in effect, smugglers, amassing for themselves — along with the financiers essential for such an operation — vast fortunes.

Not surprisingly, most chose the latter option — a choice of fabulous benefit to go-ahead young bankers like Abraham and Joseph with their symbol of a crane standing astride a globe and the words 'I watch'. Hand over fist money poured in, and for a few years an illicit trade with England flourished. It can have been little more than knowing which officials to bribe. Coffee, tea, leather-ware, iron, all continued to flow through Germany to their various markets.

Some even found their way into the French protectorate, and

Mendelssohn's birthplace in Hamburg.

17

there seems every reason to suppose that — by a supreme irony of history — the French army marched in 1812 to its defeat at Borodino in boots made from English leather.

Only in 1811 did Bonaparte take action, sending the notorious Marshal Davôut to remedy (or, as, George R. Marek suggests, to milk) the situation. In any event, it seemed prudent for certain families, among them the Mendelssohns, to leave and, their coffers groaning literally beneath the weight of their newly multiplied fortune, Abraham and Lea quickly made their way to Berlin and a house on Neue Promenade. There, on 30 October, 1813 was born Paul, the youngest son.

In Berlin, Abraham found himself so highly thought of that he was elected to the city's Municipal Council; difficult enough for anyone, unheard of hitherto for a Jew.

Their security assured, Abraham and Lea had only one further problem to solve. Should they continue faithful to the Jewish religion to which they were born or, as Lea's staid brother Jakob persistently declared, convert to the Protestant Church?

Prompted by Jakob, by birth a Salomon but now, of choice, Herr Bartholdy:

The name Bartholdy was that of the owner of a large riverside garden in Berlin that Jakob bought. If he thought this piece of ancestry by purchase would somehow hide his Jewishness, he was wrong. If anything, it made it more obvious, and Berliners used caustically to refer to his 'Jew Garden'.

Lea was the more anxious to make the change. Abraham seems, by contrast, not to have felt strongly about the matter.

At first, he went only half-way. Recognizing that conversion might help his children, all were baptized under the name Mendelssohn-Bartholdy. On a visit to Frankfurt in 1822, Abraham and Lea were also baptized Christians, although the confusion and dissent the affair caused among the Mendelssohn children was considerable. Rebecka for a time refused even to answer the name 'Bartholdy', writing she was 'Mendelssohn *nicht (not)* Bartholdy'. Fanny cross-examined her father while, out of the handful of disagreements between Felix and his father, the two most nearly acrimonious arose over the superscription foisted upon the family by Uncle Jakob.

Abraham argued that he had done little more than his father before him, 'Moses of Dessau' coining a new name when he climbed from obscurity to a position of eminence. But for Felix, the explanation never held water and, early on, he quietly dropped the Bartholdy, along with its hyphen, from his name.

Chapter 2

Childhood and Youth

'Imagine my joy, if we survive, to see the boy living in fulfilment of all his childhood gives promise of' — ZELTER, to Goethe

In differing degrees, all four Mendelssohn children were musical. The eldest, Fanny, developed into a fine pianist and a neatly accomplished composer. Only family disapproval and the conventions of the day prevented full development of her abilities. She might, at thirteen, delight her father by playing from memory a number of preludes from Bach's *The Well-Tempered Clavier,* but music was no future for a lady. The youngest, Rebecka and Paul, though less gifted, learned to sing and play various instruments.

Yet amid all this ability, it was Felix who, from the start, was the glorious exception, the glittering jewel in the Mendelssohn family's crown.

The Mendelssohns' family house in Berlin.

Top: Felix's Parents, Lea
and Abraham.
Middle: Friedrich and
Dorothea von Schlegel,
Felix's Aunt.
Centre: Rebecka Dirichlet,
Felix's younger sister.
Bottom: Wilhelm and
Fanny Hensel, Felix's
elder sister.

His musical progress was not, as we shall see, entirely without
hindrance. Love music as they did, Abraham and Lea were not convinced until quite late in their son's development that it was a
career fit for a gentleman.

Music, like all the arts, was, however, to be encouraged, and from
the beginning enjoyed an important place in the children's educational regime. Conforming to principles laid down by Humboldt,
the Prussian Minister for Education, this was itself unusual,
enlightenment and severity rubbing shoulders in equal measure.

Young Felix conducts, watched by his sister, Fanny.

Felix playing the piano. Lithograph after a pencil drawing by Wilhelm Hensel, 1821.

The children did not go to school but, rising before dawn, were taught at home by a succession of tutors. Brainwork, gymnastics, and the arts, all were to be balanced one with the other, with the aim of developing a rounded personality.

The *Hauslehrer*, fulfilling a similar function to that performed years before by Moses in the silk merchant's home, was Ludwig Heise, a distinguished philologist, and father of the poet Paul. Ludwig Berger, a pupil of Clementi taught the children piano:*
Carl Henning and Eduard Rietz, principals in the Royal Berlin Orchestra, taught violin and viola (though Mendelssohn remained, first and last, a pianist, his expertise in string writing owed much to these two childhood teachers). A quaint little professor from Berlin's prestigious Academy, the little Rössl', introduced the children to landscape sketching and drawing. Horse-riding, dancing, swimming, and outdoor games were encouraged.

Two teachers were especially influential in shaping Felix's development. The first was Adolf Bernhard Marx, a dialectician of music, gifted and tempestuous, though, as a composer, conservative and unadventurous. Abraham seems to have disliked Marx (to Eduard Devrient he wrote 'people who talk so much but produce so little' were a poor influence) but Felix listened to Marx and warned his young charge against succumbing to the pitfalls of adulation. He introduced him to the music of Beethoven and was, in time, to offer practical advice to the sixteen-year-old composer as he worked

* When Felix was fifteen, pianist and composer Ignaz Moscheles (like the Mendelssohns, a Jew) travelled to Berlin from London to hear Felix play, marvelled, and agreed to give him lessons. After a handful, he gave up, declaring 'I can teach him nothing more'. Later, the two collaborated on an amusing set of piano-duet variations on the Gypsy March from Weber's *Preciosa*.

at his *A Midsummer Night's Dream* Overture. Only later did the relationship turn sour. Following some tactless remarks by Felix about a new oratorio Marx had just composed, the older man left the room without a word, took the first stage back to Berlin and threw every letter he had received from his pupil into the Tiergarten lake. They never met again.

Far the most lasting influence was that of Carl Friedrich Zelter, hand-picked by Abraham as Felix's general music instructor, and a remarkable, if extraordinary, individual.

At fifty-nine, Director of Berlin's prestigious *Singakademie*, Zelter was among the most distinguished academic musicians of the day. The self-taught son of a stonemason, he turned to music only after an injury sustained in assisting his father had brought to an end his proposed career as a craftsman.

Karl Friedrich Zelter (1758-1832). Berlin musician, teacher of Mendelssohn.

22

It says much for Abraham's perception that he saw in this rough diamond, the master for his son's burgeoning talent. For Zelter, a learned and sensitive man devoted to the music of Bach and Handel, was a 'character'. So concerned was he not to be considered 'arty', that often he laid on ruffian manners. In company, no matter how lofty, it was only a matter of minutes before Zelter said something coarse. To those who did not know him, he must have appeared boorish. To friends able to see beneath the mask, he was a tall, burly man with a keen eye, who knew much but pretended to know little.

So highly was Zelter regarded, that this man who dressed anyhow in labourer's clothes could number among his friends celebrities as diverse as the philosopher Hegel and the playright Schiller. Towering above his contemporaries in the range and depth of his achievement, Zelter's closest friend was none other than the 'sage of Weimar', *Jupiter tonans* Johann Wolfgang von Goethe:

...that subtle and diamantine genius, the rays of his mind illuminating the most diverse subjects, the man who could turn from the incomparable lyric poetry to an enquiry into the theory of colour or the descent of man, the diplomat who inhaled and exhaled the air of the courts as if it were mountain air, the master of supple language.

Musically, Zelter's tastes were backward-looking. Bach and Haydn he loved, but thought Weber's *Der Freischütz* a joke, and for some time felt Beethoven was an awkward composer, like Hercules 'using his club to kill flies'. Schubert he ignored, while he disliked Marx and his music enough to write to Goethe a characteristically unbuttoned letter surmising that Marx must have been baptized with soda water, 'for his shit is grey-green. Like a fly he stains even the food he enjoys'.

Such was the man, however, to whom Abraham entrusted his son's musical education. In the event, it turned out to be an inspired choice. Zelter knew just how to stimulate the interest of an impish, imaginative boy. He would set Felix riddles that made the study of such dusty subjects as counterpoint a teasing game. The lessons began when Felix was eight, and as late as 1835, by which time he had become famous, we find Abraham reminding his son that 'without a shadow of a doubt your musical education would have taken quite another path without Zelter'.

Felix progressed by leaps and bounds. At nine, he appeared for the first time on the concert platform as pianist in a horn sonata by Wöffl. A year or so later he began to compose; not just isolated works, but a stream, one pouring out after the other — fugues, songs, trios, sonatas, part-songs, cantatas, operettas, little operas, a violin concerto, two piano concertos, a piano quartet (which he published as his Opus 1), and — most impressively — a series of twelve short, but often original, symphonies.

Much, to be sure, was prentice work, reflecting a young composer's delight in juggling various forms and solving problems. But the level of craftsmanship is high, sometimes astonishingly so, while every now and again there crops up a melodic or harmonic twist characteristic of the mature composer. At eleven, Felix made the first entry in what was eventually to grow to forty-four volumes, each bound in green leather, in which he meticulously listed each of his compositions. Here, it seemed, was a young man truly in earnest.

Reluctant though his parents were to acknowledge their son as a musical prodigy, his industry and enthusiasm could not be ignored. Nor could the fine finish of the results. Fortunately, the opportunities for home music-making were everything, and more a budding composer could not desire. Whether at the home on Neue Promenade or, later, a princely mansion surrounded by parkland at 3 Leipzigerstrasse, the family home had rooms always spacious enough for concerts and *soirées* on a lavish scale.

Even when Felix was very small, it was family tradition to give, every other Sunday morning, a musical party. So famous did these become, that few public figures passed through Berlin without arranging an invitation to what Heine called 'Palazzo Bartholdy'. Hegel, Ranke, the Humboldt brothers, Tieck, Heine, Hoffmann, Weber, Varnhagen, Jacob Grimm — all were there.

For Felix, these gatherings meant a valuable extension to his consuming interest. When he was not conducting a small orchestra, he would play violin or piano, sometimes alone, more often with Fanny, while Rebecka sang and Paul played the cello. He additionally composed music for the concerts, and had the great advantage of hearing new works performed almost as soon as they were finished. With Zelter on hand to advise and criticise, he could hardly fail to develop prodigiously.

At the same time, Felix developed a knack for making friends, many much older than himself. There was Karl Klingemann, eleven years his senior and, in time, secretary to the Hanovarian Legation in London. Eduard Devrient, eight years Felix's senior, became a successful actor, singer and playright, and eventually director of the Dresden Theatre. Julius Schubring, about the same age as Felix, became a prominent theologian. Gustav Droysen achieved fame as a historian, his writings on Alexander the Great, and his *History of Hellenism* influencing the later work of Mommsen and Burckhardt.

Clearly there was no resisting this serious but exuberant boy, with his long hair falling over his shoulders, his coal-black eyes, and his soft, hesitant voice. Years later, Devrient remembered the eleven-year-old Mendelssohn's appearance as he first took his place in the Friday morning singing classes at the *Singakademie*:

…among the grown-ups in his child's dress, a tight-fitting jacket cut very low at the neck, over which the wide trousers were buttoned; into the slanting pockets of these the little fellow liked to thrust his hands, rocking his curly head from side to side, and shifting restlessly from one foot to the other.

The following year, Weber was walking through the streets of Berlin with his English pupil Julius Benedict, when a boy ran up

Opening of the First
Movement of
Mendelssohn's Quartet in
E flat, written at the age
of 11. (British Museum).

and introduced himself as Felix Mendelssohn. Weber was already
late for a rehearsal of *Der Freischütz,* but Benedict allowed himself
to be dragged off to 3 Leipzigerstrasse to play through excerpts
from Weber's newly-completed opera. In return, Felix played some
Bach fugues and Cramer studies. Calling at the house a few days
later, Benedict found Felix at work on what may have been his
Opus 1:

I found him on a footstool, before a small table, writing with great earnestness. On
my asking what he was about, he replied, gravely, 'I am finishing my new Quartet
for piano and stringed instruments'. Benedict's memory may have been at fault.

According to Mendelssohn, the C Minor Quartet was only begun at Sécheron, in Switzerland, the following year. I could not resist my boyish curiosity to examine this composition and, looking over his shoulder, saw as beautiful a score as if it had been written by the most skilful copyist. It was his first Quartet in C minor. Then, forgetting quartets and Weber, down we went into the garden, he clearing high hedges with a leap, running, singing, and climbing up the trees like a squirrel.

Other childish exploits included the occasion when Felix clambered onto the roof one night, and howled like a tom cat. On another, he jammed a banana through the window of an aristocratic Polish lady's house. One acquaintance recalled playing marbles with him in a Berlin street.

With his brother and sisters, he took over the garden house at 3 Leipzigerstrasse in which the *A Midsummer Night's Dream* Overture was to be written, and produced a line and ink family newspaper; in the summer, *The Garden Paper*, in the winter, *The Tea and Snow Times*. Anyone was free to contribute, pens and paper being always to hand in this cubby hole nestling in trees at the end of the garden.

By the time he reached his twelfth birthday, Felix's energy seems to have been difficult to contain, and it was then that Zelter engineered perhaps the single most fruitful meeting of Mendelssohn's life. For in the October of that year, we find Zelter writing to Goethe:

Tomorrow morning I depart with Doris [Zelter's daughter] and a young, lively boy of twelve, my pupil, son of Herr Mendelssohn. I would love to show Doris and my best pupil to you before I depart this world. He is a good, handsome boy, spirited but obedient. His father has made the children learn something real, and with considerable effort on his part he educated them in the right way.

Mendelssohn aged 13. Drawing by Wilhelm Hensel.

That the old man agreed to see Zelter's 'best pupil', says much for the amity of their relationship. At seventy-two preoccupied with a passionate, hopeless affair with a girl of seventeen, the ageing poet had had more than his share of protégés. More than ever, he needed the tranquility of his summer house if the second, most speculative part of *Faust* was to be completed.

At the same time, Goethe's lifelong curiosity in everything around him remained undimmed, and he was evidently more than usually willing to meet this 'something special' of which his friend wrote.

The prospect of such an event, threw the Mendelssohn household into a state of excitement. His father was at pains to warn him to 'sit properly and behave nicely, especially at table. Speak clearly and sensibly and try to keep to the point'. Fanny was insistent that he keep his eyes and ears open, and threatened that 'if you cannot repeat every word that falls from his lips, I'll have nothing more to do with you'. In the rush before Felix's departure, Lea found time to write proudly her sister-in-law:

Imagine, the little scamp is to have the good luck of going to Weimar with Zelter. He wants to show him to Goethe! You'll understand what it costs me to part from the dear child, even for a few weeks. But I consider it such an advantage for him to be introduced to Goethe, to live under his roof and to receive his blessing. I am also glad of this little trip as a change for him; for his impulsiveness sometimes makes him work harder than he ought to at his age.

For Felix the trip did indeed prove an experience of the first importance. The 'little scamp' kept his promise to Fanny, and in early November sent home the first of numerous letters describing the visit:

Now listen, all of you. Today is Tuesday. On Sunday the Sun of Weimar — Goethe — appeared. In the morning we went to church, where they gave us half of Handel's 100th Psalm. The organ is large, but weak — the Marien-Kirche organ, small as it is, is much more powerful. This one has fifty stops! Afterwards I went to the Elephant Inn, where I sketched the house of Lucas Cranach. Two hours later Professor Zelter called and said: 'Goethe is here — the old man has arrived'. In a flash we were down the steps and in Goethe's house. He was in the garden and just coming round a hedge. He is very friendly, but I don't think any of the pictures are like him. One would never take him for seventy-three but fifty.

Johann Wolfgang von Goethe (1749-1832). Bust from the Goethe Memorial in Vienna.

Jacob's Ladder, a silhouette by Adele Schopenhauer, given by her to Felix during his visit to Goethe at Weimar, for his scrapbook.

Later the same day Felix played for Goethe, starting with some Bach fugues before improvising. His excitement was reflected in his playing, for a surprised Zelter (according to the poet and critic Ludwig Rellstab, who was also there) is said to have grumbled at Felix, 'What goblins and dragons are chasing you today?'. Felix also played for Goethe the minuet from *Don Giovanni*, and the overture to *The Marriage of Figaro*.

At first Goethe had not, it seems, been inclined to take this latest *wunderkind* too seriously, but such was the quality of Felix's playing that Goethe soon produced precious manuscripts for him to tackle. First came an adagio by Mozart, then some Beethoven, an all but indecipherable, ink-spattered setting of a poem of Goethe's.

In the course of the next fourteen days, the two became as close as it is possible for a precocious twelve-year-old to come to an old and venerable master. Goethe kept his young visitor busy at the piano. 'I haven't heard you yet today', he would remark, 'make a little noise for me'. Felix wrote to his parents:

I play here much more than I do at home: rarely less than four hours, sometimes six or even eight. (Goethe) sits down beside me and when I have finished (I usually improvise) I ask for a kiss or take one. You cannot imagine how good and kind he is to me.

When the time came for Felix finally to depart, Goethe gave him a generous supply of gifts, including a specially-composed poem as an accompaniment to some fanciful silhouettes that had been cut for Felix's amusement by Adele Schopenhauer.

If witches' broomsticks thus can bound
Over the solemn score,
Ride on! through wider fields of sound,
Delight us more and more,
As you have done with might and main,
And soon return to us again.

28

Though the visit to Weimar was his first real journey away from home, Felix was no stranger to travel. A few years earlier, he had sojourned with his father and Fanny as far afield as Paris, where brother and sister received a few lessons from Marie Bigot, friend and pupil of Beethoven. A year after his meeting with Goethe, Felix and the entire family set off for Switzerland, although for Felix the journey ended almost before it had begun, when he managed to get lost at the first stop, Potsdam.

When they at last arrived, Switzerland had on Felix a lasting impact. As usual, the four children (who were attended throughout the four-month vacation by a battery of tutors) took out their sketchbooks and began recording every view in sight. Felix found time also to write long letters to his friends in Berlin, in which he described the new sights and sounds he had discovered. Zelter was treated to an account of Swiss yodelling, replete with music examples jotted on the spot.

'This kind of singing', Felix wrote, 'sounds harsh and unpleasant when it is heard nearby, or in a room ... it consists of notes which are produced from the throat and generally is made up from ascending sixths ... in the valleys, the mountains or the woods when you hear it mingling with the answering echoes, it sounds beautiful'. His ear was, however, affronted by what he heard in the Bernese Oberland. Here, much to Felix's indignation, the girls were accustomed to sing in parallel fifths, thus breaking one of the sacred rules of polite music.

The outward route from Berlin had included a number of musical stopovers. Armed with a letter of introduction from Zelter, the family met in Cassel the composer Louis Spohr. In Frankfurt, they met the pianist Ferdinand Hiller, two years Felix's junior, and soon to become a friend. On the return home, Felix kept a promise to Goethe of the previous fall, and the whole family stayed for a short time at Weimar. Felix's return was, Goethe suggested, like the young David come to cheer Saul with his music.

Only at long last did the family arrive back at 3 Leipzigerstrasse, Felix busying himself with his latest one act opera, *The Uncle from Boston*. As soon as it was ready for performance, a small stage was erected in the family's largest drawing room.

After the first performance, Zelter stood before the audience and, turning to his fourteen-year-old protégé, said, 'My dear boy, from this day you are no longer an apprentice, but a full member of the brotherhood of musicians. I hereby proclaim you independent in the name of Mozart, Haydn and old father Bach'.

For all the magnitude of his son's achievement, Abraham, however, still had qualms. As for Felix's uncle, the prim little Jakob Bartholdy, there could be no question that there were few occupations less fitting a young man of rank than music. Who, he argued, could in any case be certain that Felix's youthful brilliance, however pronounced now, would not fade with maturity? What then?

In the end, Abraham decided to consult the single best musician he knew, the testy but perceptive composer and pedagogue, Luigi Cherubini. If Cherubini thought Felix had the makings of a first-class musician, he would be allowed to continue. If not, Abraham would insist that he turn to something else.

Confident that all would be well, Felix fell in with his father's plans, and in the summer of 1824 the two set out for Paris and Cherubini.

Far from being overawed by the trip, Felix was highly responsive to everyone and everything that came his way, his letters home flowing thick and fast. For the first time, he saw and met the leading lights of contemporary music. On the whole, he was not impressed, though once or twice one senses his youthful impetuosity getting the better of him.

'Liszt', he reported to Fanny, 'plays very well, he has splendid fingers, but no brains'. Meyerbeer fared no better, '(He) gave a lecture on the nature of the horn. I laughed so much I nearly fell off the chair'. Rossini, the depressive genius who hid his brilliance behind a façade of drollery and indifference, was 'the great Maestro Windbag'. Auber, 'a grey haired old man, pupil of Cherubini and darling of the public ought at least be able to orchestrate, especially in our times, when the publication of Mozart, Haydn and Beethoven scores has made it so easy!'.

Hall of the Paris Conservatoire.

Maria Luigi Cherubini (1760-1842). Director of the Paris Conservatoire.

Felix rose high on a wave of optimism. Not even the prospect of meeting Cherubini disturbed him. He had concluded already that his judge was, creatively, 'an extinct volcano, still throwing occasional sparks and flashes, but quite buried in ash and stones', and although the old man had a reputation for being difficult to please, one doubts whether Felix was at all surprised when Cherubini, after listening carefully to the piano quartet, said simply to Abraham, 'Your boy is talented. He will do well. He has already done well'.

'He will do well' — did Cherubini in later years ever ponder the clairvoyance of these words? From the age of ten, Felix had been active as a composer. His music had grace, charm and spontaneity. Yet, less than a year after his audience with Cherubini, he had, in one of music's miracles, leapt at one step to maturity.

How it is difficult to comprehend, yet there the evidence is. For in 1825, at just sixteen, Felix Mendelssohn wrote down, at white heat, his Octet for strings.

Crystallized in one short span here is a talent something far more than merely precocious, one that has as well as easy brilliance, depth and maturity.

31

The Octet, as Hans Keller has suggested, is perhaps the single most astounding achievement of any child composer. At sixteen, even Mozart and Schubert produced nothing finer.

Of the work's four movements, the most original is the third, a *scherzo* to be played, the composer requests, 'quickly and very finely'. According to Fanny, Felix here attempted to capture the atmosphere of the witches' revels in Goethe's *Faust:*

> *Scudding cloud and misty mead,*
> *Are tinged with light of day,*
> *Gusts in the leaves and wind in the reeds,*
> *And all is blown away.*

The Octet was an immediate success, Felix himself making a piano-duet arrangement and an orchestral version. Years later, he admitted that the Octet, still his favourite work, had been 'a joy' to write.

It was no surprise that Felix discussed the background to the music with Fanny. From the start, there existed between brother and sister a bond of love and understanding. When Felix was thirteen, Fanny wrote, 'I have watched his progress step by step and think I have contributed to his development. He never writes anything down before submitting it to my critical judgement — I have known his operas note for note before anything was written down'.

When, months after finishing the Octet, Felix announced that he had completed an overture to Shakespeare's *A Midsummer Night's Dream* it was, however, Marx who could best say that he had watched it grow, bar by bar. Having criticised an earlier draft, Marx wrote:

He (Felix) suggested accepting my suggestions, and the overture assumed its present form. At the first performance his father went so far as to say that the overture was really *my* work! This was, of course, quite untrue. The ideas and the execution are his. I was only a critic.

Here was Felix's second masterpiece. Schumann wrote that 'the bloom of youth lies over it. In an inspired moment, the mature master took his first and loftiest flight'. And, as an English musicologist concisely put it, 'With *A Midsummer Night's Dream* we cannot think of Shakespeare without Mendelssohn, or Mendelssohn without Shakespeare'. Wilfred Blunt remarks that neither in Verdi's *Otello* nor his *Falstaff*, in Vaughan Williams' *Sir John in Love*, or in Elgar's *Falstaff*, was the essence of Shakespeare captured so completely.

When Felix and Fanny in November played Moscheles the duet arrangement, he could write only that this 'great and still youthful genius has once again made gigantic strides forward'.

Thereafter, Abraham's brightest 'King of the Moors' scarcely looked back. Attending Hegel's lectures on aesthetics and submitting a translation of Terence's *Andria,* he matriculated successfully from Berlin University.

Gasparo Spontini (1774-1851). Chief Director of Music in Berlin for more than 20 years, retiring in 1842.

Spontini.

Berlin University.
(Mary Evans Library).

At Frankfurt, Hiller failed for a moment to recognise the dandy that hailed him 'in a tall shiny hat. He had changed a lot. His figure had filled out. There was a general smartness about him. He had grown into a man'.

Not even the failure of a further attempt at opera, *Camacho's Wedding*, cunningly sabotaged by the musical director of the Royal Opera, Gasparo Spontini, could dent Felix's optimism. As he later told Devrient, even 'the most brilliant praise of the best newspaper hasn't much power to gratify'.

The future held riches. His enthusiasm for Bach, always high, had intensified of late. Parting from the musicologist Justus Thibaut he declared, 'Farewell, we'll build our friendship on Luis da Vittoria and Sebastian Bach!'.

Chapter 3

The St. Matthew Passion

'History will recompense his deed with fame, as his contemporaries who were privileged to witness the work will offer him warm thanks and honour' — Adolf MARX

Until quite recently, it was a commonplace of musical history that in the half century since his death, Johann Sebastian Bach — a figure regarded by smart Parisians, wrote the sixteen-year-old Mendelssohn, as 'a powdered wig, stuffed with learning' — had fallen into the sea of oblivion; a slough of neglect from which he was rescued only in 1829 when, like Astynax, the young man from Hamburg saved the day and brought to life for the first time in a hundred years the mighty *St. Matthew Passion*.

The facts, however, read a little differently. Bach had never been entirely forgotten. Too difficult for use in ordinary services, his smaller church works were admired nonetheless by theologians with musical leanings. Moscheles and Czerny presented various of the keyboard works. In Vienna, a chamber group staged at least one complete performance of the *Brandenburg* Concertos. Every organist worthy of the name would have known most if not all Bach's most important works for the instrument. Zelter's *Singakademie* choir sang certain of the motets at their Friday morning gatherings (Zelter himself had been a pupil of Johann Kimberger, a student of Bach's), while the young Beethoven is said to have soothed Baron von Swieten during the quiet watches of the night by playing Bach fugues. Then as now, the instrumental works enjoyed much popularity whenever a few friends could be drawn together for an evening's music-making.

Far from being forgotten, 'Old Sebastian' was known and revered by most discriminating musicians. The public at large on the other hand, *had* fallen out of touch with Bach's music, and there can be no denying that in the years following the composer's death the great tapestries of the Passions, the Oratorios and the Masses had languished all but forgotten — something that had less to do with the public's inability to grasp the music's complexities than the fact that essential manuscripts were generally inaccessible to concert

Baron Gottfried von Swieten

34

Johann Sebastian Bach
(1685-1750).

organisations, lying instead in museums, monasteries, and other dusty catacombs of neglect.

In 1802, however, the first biography of the Leipzig cantor — Forkel's — appeared. Shortly after, E.T.A. Hoffman issued a panegyric to this 'genius of mankind'. One of Germany's most widely read authors and, in his fantastical way, in the forefront of the growing romantic movement, Hoffman's was a voice to be respected. With no less a figure than Weber adding his weight to the argument, the time was evidently ripe for a Bach revival on the grand scale.

Yet between conception and reality there yawned a considerable gap. To visualise a renewal of interest in Bach's most monumental works was one thing. To carry such a project through was another. For a start, manuscript sources had first to be drawn together and sorted into some kind of order. Having grappled with that particular bees' nest, who was on hand to mastermind works such as the Passions, with their grand gestures, their counterpoint, their involved choruses and their panoply of soloists. A half century was in any case a long time. News travelled slowly, memories were short, and the performing tradition established by Bach had been

Leopold Mozart
(1719-87); Frontispiece to
first edition of his *Violin
School*, 1756.

largely lost from view. As Leopold Mozart, father of Wolfgang Amadeus, wrote, 'With old music one arrives at so many differing conclusions — everything is really very confusing'.

Manuscripts, as we have seen, had first to be released from bondage. Here, Zelter is of particular importance. As one of the first researchers active in the field, he devoted much time to digging up chips of Bach — often from the most outlandish sources — and then (with the true collector's glee) locking himself in his study to ponder them in candle-lit solitude (Zelter was apparently given to secreting manuscripts in a large commode, in front of which he would strike suitably theatrical poses. No doubt this was the resting place of some valuable Bach manuscripts once given him by Abraham).

Elsewhere, Frenchman Georg Poelchau was no less avid a collector, with a prize selection of coveted Bachiana. The name Bach clearly carried a deal of prestige, and it is interesting to find Adolf Marx recalling that:

As a matter of course I spoke to one and all who would listen to me. That is how old Schlesinger the publisher heard about the *St. Matthew Passion*. He asked who the publisher was. It had never been published. 'Then I will publish it', he exclaimed, and at once the printing of the full score and of the piano reduction was decided. His associates were of a different opinion and tried to throttle the project. The old man, with his lion voice, banged the table. 'Even if it were to cost me 3,000 thaler I would do it for the prestige of our firm'. The *Passion* was published.

So even if his works were considered dry and 'prickly', Bach was by no means the forgotten colossus. As for the *St. Matthew Passion*, Zelter himself owned what he thought was the manuscript.

At this point, it is possible to clear away two stories. The first, originally put out by Devrient, is that Zelter bought the manuscript — it was, in fact, only a reasonably faithful copy — from a merchant who had used the pages for wrapping cheese. Far from finding its way onto some unmusical cheesemonger's shelf, Zelter's manuscript, along with one or two other copies, had long been preserved carefully and catalogued. Indeed, by 1828 its existence was widely known enough for two publishers to contemplate rival editions. There was no mystery — the *Passion* was merely unpublished and not easily available.

The second tale concerns Mendelssohn's acquisition of what is usually supposed to have been Zelter's closely-guarded copy. Felix's grandmother Babette is here alleged to have wanted to give Felix as a Christmas gift a manuscript with which he would be unfamiliar. Musical, and in her time a favourite pupil of Bach's youngest son, Wilhelm Friedmann, the old lady knew of the *Passion* and is supposed to have written to Zelter demanding his copy. Zelter, the story goes, refused, causing Babette to stress pointedly that the Mendelssohns were contributing generously to his beloved *Singakademie*.

Might it not, all things considered, be better if he co-operated?

Philipp Eduard Devrient (1801-77), German opera singer. Friend and biographer of Mendelssohn.

Thus is the *St. Matthew Passion* supposed to have been wheedled from the *Singakademie* chief and presented to his no doubt dazzled pupil.

As modern research confirms, Babette indeed gave Felix a manuscript copy of the *Passion* at Christmas, 1823. But the score from which he subsequently worked, glossed with Felix's annotations, indicates that it was *not* Zelter's copy that had been obtained but Poelchau's. As Martin Geck writes, this is all the more likely when we recall that Poelchau was a friend of Babette Salomon and her husband, and a frequent house guest. Zelter did not refuse. He was never asked.

Whatever the origin of the text, its advent was a major event in Felix's life and he so immersed himself in its music that the *Passion* soon became a corner-stone of his existence. Burning with enthusiasm the eighteen-year-old Mendelssohn, during the winter of 1827/8, led a small group of amateurs through a number of domestic performances at 3 Leipzigerstrasse. Thérèse Devrient, who took part, wrote:

(Felix's) mother sent invitations to about twelve people, the sisters copying the voice parts so that we could begin — however modestly — at least with serious

37

intent. Felix would sit at the piano, pale and excited. We the singers stood around him so that he could at all times see us. That was very necessary. Not only did we experience difficulty in singing the music by sight, but both the notes and the text were so illegible that it was almost impossible to make sense out of them. Yet we were terribly moved and felt that we had been transported into a new world of music.

This, according to Thérèse, happened in October 1828. At the New Year, 1829 a further performance was given of the first section alone, after which Eduard Devrient, who had sung the role of Jesus, recorded that he went home in a state of high excitement.

In a moment, it seems, he concluded that a public performance of the *Passion* was a necessity (the account that follows is Devrient's own). Such was Devrient's impatience that first thing the following morning he was banging at the front door of 3 Leipzigerstrasse, demanding an audience with his friend. Felix, Paul assured him, was still asleep, but agreeing it was time that he was woken began that difficult operation (only after he had been shaken, shouted at and generally prodded was it ever possible to rouse the sleeping Felix. On this occasion, he must have been perplexed to find not just his younger brother but an anxious Devrient waiting by his bedside).

Devrient had, he said, something of vital importance to discuss, bursting out quickly his proposal that the *Passion* be staged without further delay at the *Singakademie*. Felix's first reaction was

The Singakademie, Berlin.

38

disbelieving laughter, but Devrient, nothing deterred, proceeded to elaborate. The *Passion,* he argued, was the greatest and most important monument of German music. It was their artistic duty to revive it, a task for which Felix was the only choice. The *Singakademie,* Devrient continued, owed him a break. For some years he had worked for its advancement, and they could hardly refuse him something on which his heart was set.

After some thought, Felix replied that Devrient was probably right, and that he provisionally approved his plan that they tackle the venture together. 'But', he added, 'nothing will come of it because Zelter will object. He thinks a performance is impossible, simply because he hasn't summoned up the courage to try the music himself. He thinks it's indigestible'.

Devrient was, however, insistent, arguing that if necessary he was prepared to go over Zelter's head and appeal direct to the *Singakademie* trustees — a move Felix wisely refused to countenance. The friends agreed accordingly to visit Zelter and lay their plans before him, Mendelssohn warning Devrient in advance that 'if he turns nasty, I'll leave. I simply can't stand bickering'.

When they walked in, Zelter, seated at his piano, was at first genial. He expressed pleasant surprise that two such fine young men should visit him at such an early hour. The swan quill he still used for writing, Devrient recalled, was resting between his fingers, his large frame engulfed in a cloud of smoke that issued from his gnarled pipe. The two ran through their plans, Zelter (as usual, when agitated) soon striding up and down the room, giving tongue to all the counter-arguments Felix had expected. The *Passion,* he declared, needed greater performing skill than was to be had at the time, more especially choirs with the kind of flexibility found among those trained by Bach himself. In addition, he warned them, a performance would require a double orchestra of the highest standard, with especially competent string players. Long and arduous rehearsals would be necessary. In short, had it been a realistic possibility, all four Passions would have been revived long ago.

Felix and Eduard then expanded their case, pinning their argument on the fine quality of Zelter's *Singakademie* choir and the fact that, having worked privately on the score for a year and more, they could muster between them enough skill and enthusiasm to ensure a successful performance.

At this point, Zelter, used to having his word taken as gospel, seems to have lost his temper, and the two friends started to edge towards the door, Felix, Devrient recalled, looking especially distraught. Indeed, he already had his hand on the doorknob when, without warning Zelter just as quickly calmed down and tried to employ reason rather than emotion to support his case. The trustees would have to give their consent. That, he felt, was unlikely. There were, moreover, ten women on the board and Felix surely knew what *they* were like. The women would certainly regard the *St. Matthew Passion* as too much like hard work. 'Ten

39

Anna Milder-Hauptmann
(1785-1838).

come to a rehearsal', Zelter tartly observed, 'and tomorrow twenty stay away'.

Yet so insistent were the two friends that finally, in exasperation, the *Singakademie's* thorny director grudgingly capitulated: 'In God's name, alright! I can't fight the two of you. See what you can do'. Devrient and Mendelssohn rushed out into the street, exulting and shaking hands with each other. 'To think', Felix exclaimed, 'that an actor and a Jew should give back to the people the greatest Christian music in the world'. It was the only time, Devrient wrote, that Mendelssohn ever mentioned his Jewish origins.

Although Devrient's account rings true, it leaves unanswered a number of questions. Why, for example, did Zelter, the great Bach champion, so vehemently oppose their plans? Zelter had a fair degree of vanity, but was first and last a musician with a deep love of Bach, and hardly a man to turn up, in a fit of pique, the chance of hearing the first performance in a century of one of his hero's greatest works.

More likely, he doubted even his brightest pupil's ability as a twenty-year-old to command the huge forces needed for such an occasion. Likely to, that he knew that Spontini, along with certain members of the Royal Berlin Orchestra, abhorred Mendelssohn as a rich man's son, a dilettante and amateur, and a Jew; and that they along with audiences more accustomed to snowy-haired *kapellmeisteren,* would give his pupil (and, by implication, himself and his *Singakademie)* a rough ride.

Zelter had nonetheless a measure of courage, and gave the project his blessing. Felix and Devrient, for their part, threw themselves into the necessary preparations, the concert being arranged as a charity gala in aid of the quaintly-named 'Sewing School for Indigent Girls' (so charitable did the event become that the Mendelssohns had themselves to pay for the hire of the hall, while Felix forbore to charge any fee at all).

Having selected their soloists, the two friends approached each individually (the soprano they decided, was to be Maria Milder-Hauptmann, Beethoven's first Leonore and, according to Haydn, blessed with a voice 'as big as a house'). Well to the fore among Felix's characteristics was his mania for tidiness. This, coupled with an infectious enthusiasm and a deep understanding of the music, enabled rehearsals to proceed with maximum efficiency. These were soon transferred from the smaller to the larger of the *Singakademie's* two halls. The chorus finally numbered 158 (not the four or five hundred often quoted). Professional section leaders of an orchestra otherwise composed of amateurs, included Eduard Rietz and Ferdinand David from the Royal Orchestra.

If there was any animosity of the kind Zelter feared, it must have evaporated with the first run-through. Having for a time kept a wary eye on proceedings, Zelter soon withdrew from the platform altogether in favour of a seat in the hall.

There were, it is recorded, nine full rehearsals. Mendelssohn for the first time used a baton, in 1829 itself unusual. In accordance with *Singakademie* tradition, he stood at right angles to his audience in front of a diagonally placed piano.

Rumours of what was in the making soon spread. Musicians asked to be admitted to rehearsals. The *Berliner Allgemeine Musikalische Zeitung* (edited by Adolf Marx) published five analytical essays.

Felix was especially concerned that the 'right people' should attend the performance, writing for example to the *kapellmeister* of Dessau, one Friedrich Schneider, urging him to 'brave the journey' and to make inroads into his precious time by sojourning in Berlin.

Felix was also keen that even the most encouraging audience should be able to absorb so substantial a work, and although Alfred Einstein's accusation that the *Passion* was severely mutilated cannot be sustained, excisions were made and a certain amount of re-orchestration undertaken. But as far as one can judge from Mendelssohn's tempo and dynamic markings. In the score now lodged in the Bodleian Library, Oxford. The interpretation was on the whole not as theatrical as the flamboyant re-instrumentation of 'And behold, the veil of the temple' suggests. While the quick tempi Felix seems usually to have favoured may have emphasised the work's more dramatic moments, the performance seems *in toto* to have been true to the spirit of the work.

When tickets went on sale, the house was within minutes sold out. More than a thousand people clamoured in vain for admittance on the night, 11 March, 1829. The atmosphere among an audience that included the King, the poet Heine, Droysen, the theologian Schleiermacher, and Raphael Varnhagen was, according to Fanny, 'like a church ... deepest silence'.

Emotion filled the hall, a few openly weeping as Felix, poised and immaculate, moulded a realisation of Bach's score that, for all its occasional lapses of intonation and false entries, was marked by authority and fervour. The evening was by any standards a spectacular success, news of which spread across Berlin like wildfire.

A further performance was clearly a must, and duly took place ten days later, on Bach's birthday. Zelter — who by now seems to have claimed the whole idea as his own — threw a lavish supper. Sitting between Felix and a man who constantly plied her with drinks and showered her with foolish compliments, Thérèse Devrient eventually hissed to Felix, 'Who's this idiot beside me?'. 'That idiot', Mendelssohn whispered, 'is Hegel'.

Reviews were fulsome. The sometimes venemous Rellstab — he was twice arrested, once for insulting Spontini, once for upsetting the soprano Henriette Sontag — wrote of the 'eternally great, infinitely moving miraculous power and nobility' of the work. Martin Geck writes:

Never before was society so involved in, and appreciative of, a musical event. No other work of music called forth at its première or rediscovery a comparable chorus of famous contemporaries, respected critics and anonymous contributors.

Zelter sent additionally two reports to Goethe who, much moved, noted in his diary, 'Zelter's letter about Bach's music'. At the same time, he replied that he was made to feel as if he could 'hear the roar of the ocean from afar', and compared the feeling of hearing the work in the mind's eye to his emotions when he first saw Mantegna's drawings.

As if this were not enough, Zelter himself gave a third performance on Good Friday, 17 April. According to Fanny's detailed report to Felix (who by then had left Berlin) Zelter conducted so badly that Milder-Hauptmann lost her place and the chorus missed numerous cues. Whether this was wholly fair, we shall never know. Marek suggests that the letter is further evidence of Fanny's almost blind adoration of her brother — if Felix were not on hand to take charge, the performance could not conceivably be good.

Mendelssohn or no, Bach's masterpiece was bound to be heard, sooner or later. But Felix's achievement was crucial, demolishing at a stroke the fears that had for a century prevented public performances. Within a year, Schlesinger, badgered by Marx, published the score. Performances were before long given all over Germany, generally to acclaim, though a Königsberg critic recorded that at an 1832 performance 'half the audience fled during the first part, the rest called the work out-of-date rubbish'. All this Mendelssohn did without for a moment succumbing to the label 'Bach specialist'. 'Old Sebastian' he revered. He loved his music deeply. But, as he wrote his sister Rebecka, years later:

If you really feel for what is beautiful, if it truly gladdens you, then your mind becomes enlarged rather than narrowed. I always get upset when some praise only Beethoven, others only Palestrina and still others only Mozart or Bach. All four of them, I say, or none at all.

42

Chapter 4

New Horizons

'It's fearful! It's mad! I'm mixed up and confused. London is the grandest and most complicated monster on the face of the earth' — MENDELSSOHN, to his father

For the Mendelssohns, the old German admonition 'If I rest, I rust' was a motto to be paid something more than lip service. A hotbed of activity, the house at 3 Leipzigerstrasse must often have seemed like a fairground merry-go-round. In similar fashion, the whole family enjoyed travel as much as they did the pursuit of professional and social excellence.

For Felix, moving from place to place came quickly to represent a necessity of existence. As a consequence, even when there was no overriding need, he would pack his bag and depart. In accepting posts in Düsseldorf, Leipzig or Berlin, he was careful to stipulate free periods to enable him to visit distant cities, or simply to take time out to travel where he pleased.

In 1827, for example, he had already made his way to Stettin for the first public performance of *A Midsummer Night's Dream* Overture, only to decamp without warning to Heidelberg and Cologne. Soon after, he set out on a strenuous walking tour of southern Germany. In Baden, he visited a casino where he was persuaded to play the piano. This he did so successfully that the patrons, to the fury of the manager, stopped playing roulette. Never again, the manager vowed, would there be a piano in the gambling parlour.

After the *St. Matthew Passion*, Felix could hardly wait to get away from Berlin. There may have been more to this than his impatience to see something of the world. At twenty, he was still the boy next door, and Abraham and Lea probably felt it was time for him to start making his own way. So far as his career was concerned, this made sense. After the *St. Matthew Passion* there seemed little more for Felix to achieve in the Prussian capital, at least in the immediate future.

He was, besides, never completely at ease in the city. This in part had to do with the petty intrigues and vendettas of Spontini and his anti-semitic cronies. Mendelssohn, it was said, was wealthy and

43

Jewish and, after all, had never had to make his own way. Everything had been laid on for him from the cradle. According to Henry F. Chorley, an English music critic who travelled in Prussia, some even deprecated his abilities. 'Mendelssohn', they would sigh, 'ah, he had talent as a boy'.

It should also be remembered that after the success of the *St. Matthew Passion,* the King, Wilhelm III, did *not* offer Mendelssohn any kind of court post while, from a social point of view, life in Berlin was becoming daily less comfortable.

A few visitors might continue to regard the city as a 'sandy nest'. Others were less sanguine. Sophie Muller, a leading actress, left a chilly impression. Entering Berlin by the Leipziger Tor:

...a shudder came over me. It was ten o'clock at night. The streets were deathly quiet. Only an occasional light here and there showed me the city was not, like Herculaneum, uninhabited.

The playwright Heinrich Laube, active in the *New Germany* movement, minced his words even less, describing Prussia as an out-and-out police state. 'Berlin', he wrote, 'was a dead city; in considerable part of the Friedrichstadt district, grass is growing between the cobblestones'. The main street leading to Charlottenburg was the only thoroughfare on which smoking was allowed. Anyone caught smoking elsewhere was liable to a fine. As Laube was talking one day with friends, someone hissed, 'Quick, throw away your cigar — the King's behind us!'. 'There he was', Laube continues, 'in an open carriage, and hardly responded to our greeting'. 'The majority of educated men were no doubt liberally inclined, but they thought their liberalism could be made compatible with an absolute and bureaucratic government'.

Mendelssohn was not, by nature, a political animal. But, even assuming that Laube exaggerated, he can hardly have escaped the feeling that he was confined to a capital city gone largely to seed.

The flower of politics had long since withered. Stein, disappointed in his hopes for reform, had gone. Humboldt, friend of Goethe and architect of the Prussian educational system, had withdrawn from public life as early as 1819 in protest against the growing wave of reaction. By 1827, even church sermons were being scanned for subversive content.

The ageing Wilhelm, became ever more self-communing and suspicious of those around him. He refused to give his people the promised constitution, condemning all proposals for reform as 'effusions of unripe poets, destined to lead to perdition'. When he went to the theatre, a red carpet would cover his loge, hiding him from public scrutiny, the reclusive monarch relying on the Duchess of Leignitz for news of what was happening on stage. Only occasionally would he peer out to see for himself.

It was determined, then, that Felix should travel. But why London? Why not Vienna, the home of Mozart, Beethoven and Schubert? Or Paris, where Felix was already known?

Firstly, the Mendelssohns liked and approved everything British,

Karl Klingemann. Mendelssohn's friend and travelling companion on his visit to Scotland. Drawing by Wilhelm Hensel.

down to tea, which they adored (Felix had, additionally, a weakness for rice pudding). Second, Ignaz Moscheles was there. As Harold C. Schonberg has written, Moscheles, a sensitive musician, was also 'a gentleman, as noble and respected a figure as music has shown'. Full of kindness and enthusiasm, he had already befriended the young Mendelssohn, and doubtless told him of the welcome that awaited visiting artists in London. Clementi, Cramer, Dussek, Hummel — all had travelled to the English capital and been appreciated. Felix was sure to be appreciated as well.

Finally, Felix's good friend Klingemann was there, enjoying life as Secretary at the Hanovarian Legation in St. James's. For some time he had kept up a bombardment of letters detailing the pleasures of life by the Thames:

The comfort here! British comfort is the most marvellous, Philistine invention I've ever known. It begins about ten in the morning, in my small, homey little room, only half as high as the reception in the Embassy in Berlin, and very

45

pleasantly furnished. A merry fire is burning in the fireplace, the water is cooking, the breakfast table laid, and everything needed for breakfast right there. My eye scans with great satisfaction the mile-long newspaper [*The Times*] with leading articles, news, law-suits, police investigations, and all kinds of scandal. Everything is made public. Frequently, I have the impression I'm reading a comedy by Aristophanes. The coal is crackling, the coffee steaming, and between each sip I learn about an interesting elopement of a romantic young Miss, a daring burglary (by the way, thievery here is unbelievable), or a dreadful accident...

I only wish I were less short-sighted: that's because of the English girls. They don't know how to bake a cake, but how marvellous they look! They parade in pairs, the taller ones together, and are quite conscious of their charms. Even the chamber maid at Goltermann looks like a princess or a Hebe.

Regent's Park and Regent Street is truly the most impressive sight I've seen, almost more beautiful than the Linden. Best of all is the City. It's a pleasure to make one's way through the mass of carriages, coal carriers, crooks and honest folk. There's something dæmonic in this enormous, intense activity, yet somehow an order reigns without even having to invoke law.

On Sunday when one walks through the same streets in which, on workdays, you literally can't hear yourself talk, one is almost frightened by the silence. The incredible, thick yellow fog hangs over the city and penetrates into the rooms, all stores are closed, and there are no newspapers; a plaintive little bell calls the pious together...

In one respect we Germans have an advantage here: everyone thinks that all of us were born smoking a pipe and owning a piano and every German is a *priori* musical. These good people have a touching sense for music and an extraordinary stomach for listening. Like ostriches, they swallow sand and sweets together.

I'm absolutely mad about the theatre here, particularly the English comedies. The public participates more than at home, although displays a certain critical innocence. Well-declaimed speeches move it to applause and when there are jokes people really laugh at them. At the entrance to the theatre, before the doors are opened, the policemen call out, 'Gentlemen, take care of your pockets when going in — take care of pickpockets, Gentlemen!', and everybody guards his belongings. A newspaper here, *The Herald,* estimates the number of pickpockets of both sexes to be between 80 to 100 thousand.*

England, on the eve of the Victorian age, was enjoying prestige and prosperity. With French expansionism crushed, people slept in their beds more easily. The Duke of Wellington set the fashion for a true-blue Tory administration, while London was the hub of a vast financial and commercial power just beginning to climb toward its imperial zenith. The industrial revolution was centred in English factories, and the country's wealth increased steadily through massive exports of iron and coal.

Britain's political strength had meanwhile been buttressed by talents shrewdly employed as a broker in international relations. In this way, March, 1829 saw Parliament approve the long-awaited Greek protocol, allowing that country its independence, and generating a premium of goodwill.

By contrast to the bright lights glittering across the channel, Berlin must have seemed a poky, provincial place. True, English

* London at the time had been plagued by a wave of thievery, and just as Felix arrived, Sir Robert Peel managed to get approval of his plans to establish the forerunner of the Metropolitan Police Force.

music had yet to produce another creative genius of the calibre of Henry Purcell, dead and buried in Westminster Abbey for over a century. But the variety and vitality of its concert halls was unrivalled.

Handel and Haydn had in their time been virtually adopted. Handel had settled in London in 1712 and, with his music and his thundering temper, dominated the country's musical life until his death some fifty years later. Haydn had made, during the 1790s, two extended visits, his brilliant music and sweet, simple nature being lionized by the concert-going public.

Pianistic virtuosity was popular, but the largest audiences were reserved for visiting operatic stars. Between them, Maria Malibran and Giudetta Pasta crammed Covent Garden and Drury Lane. Italian opera predominated, audiences being brought to their feet nightly by sentimentality and unbelievable vocal acrobatics.

Much as English audiences welcomed visiting artists and enjoyed musical entertainments, their manners, however, often left much to be desired. Throughout the performance, gossip would often continue unabated and sweets and oranges be nibbled noisily. Patrons would come and go as they pleased, and if that meant pushing past someone or overturning with a clatter some chairs, so be it. Some people seemed scarcely to care what they saw or heard, as long as it didn't interfere with their other goings-on. Addison had scolded his theatre-going readers years earlier in *The Spectator* with the observation that:

There is no question that our great-grandchildren will be very curious to know the reason why their forefathers used to sit together like an audience of foreigners in their own country, and to hear whole plays acted before them in a tongue which they did not understand.

It has further to be admitted that, by modern standards, the concert programmes of the time look rather odd, serious items being interwoven with selections and pot-pourris from popular 'hits' of the time.

Yet the greatest jewel in musical London's crown was the London (later the Royal) Philharmonic Society. Founded in 1813, its existence indicated the demand there was for music-making of the highest quality. A brave, co-operative venture undertaken by prominent musicians including Clementi and Johann Peter Salomon (the promoter who had enticed Haydn to England), its sole aim was to present symphonic music. Only members could play and only first-class musicians could become members.

From the outset, the Society prospered. Enough money was raised to invite celebrities of the stature of Cherubini and Spontini to conduct, and to commission new works. The impoverished Beethoven had received on his flea-ridden deathbed a much appreciated gift of £100 from the Society. In addition, there were institutions devoted to orchestral music, such as 'The Concerts of Ancient Music', which specialised in old music, and Sir George Smart's

'The City Concerts'. These were founded in 1818, and consisted in the main of enthusiastic amateurs.

Smart was also a founder of the Philharmonic Society, conducting in 1825 the première of a strange and puzzling new symphony, Beethoven's Ninth. As soon as the season was ended, Smart set out on a continental tour to track down new music and to find out what up and coming performers were to be heard. In September, he called on Beethoven and tried vainly (in a conversation conducted with difficulty owing to Beethoven's by now total deafness) to persuade him to come to England.

Wherever he went, Smart carried with him a pocket tuning-fork to check that music was being played in tune. By October, Smart and his tuning-fork had found their way to Berlin. Here he was duly invited to 3 Leipzigerstrasse and, like Moscheles before him, marvelled at what he found.

Young Felix Mendelssohn played a clever fugue, pastorale and fantasia of Sebastian Bach, all on the organ with a very difficult part for the pedals. Next he played a clever *kyrie* of his own composition, the voice parts well put together but difficult. He and his two sisters played on two pianofortes an overture of his own composition, which was learned and good. (After dinner) I played Mozart's duet in F with Miss Mendelssohn, and Mozart's Fantasia with Mr. Mendelssohn junior, who also played three difficult clever exercises of his own composition.

Recording that Lea presented him with the printed rules of the *Singakademie*, and that he gave Fanny a set of Maundy pence for 1825 'which seemed to please her', Smart later said farewell to Abraham and Felix at the *Liedertafel*, a glee club for men on Mohrenstrasse:

There seemed about sixty gentlemen present. Between each dish, as they were brought round, they sang a short piece in the style of a glee, most of them composed by Zelter. Zelter is a pleasant unassuming man. One of his fingers is crooked. He was formally a mason. He said he had built ten houses in Berlin, and did not begin music before he was twenty. I strongly recommended young Mendelssohn to visit England when I was in Berlin which he then seemed inclined to do.

Here, then, were good reasons for Felix wanting to visit London, and for Abraham feeling that a change of air could be productive as well as pleasant for him. Friday, 18 April, 1829 consequently found him embarking from Hamburg on the steamship *Attwood*, his father and Rebecka having accompanied him as far as the port. Here a loving farewell from Fanny was waiting. As can be judged from the length of the crossing (Mendelssohn disembarked at noon on the Tuesday), the passage was a bad one. The engines broke down and Felix lay prostrate with sea-sickness the whole Sunday and Monday:

From Saturday evening to Monday afternoon we had contrary winds, and such a storm that all on board were ill. We had once to stop for a while on account of a dense fog, and then again in order to repair the engine; even last night at the mouth of the Thames we were obliged to cast anchor to avoid a collision with another ship. Fancy, moreover, that from Sunday morning to Monday evening I

Ignaz Moscheles (1794-1870). Brilliant pianist. Resident in London from 1826-41, when he was appointed head of the Piano Department at Leipzig University.

had one fainting fit after another, drom disgust with myself and everything about the boat, cursing England, and particularly my own *Calm Sea* and scolding the waiter with all my might.*

When eventually Felix crawled down the gangplank to find Moscheles and Klingemann waiting for him, he immediately felt better. Moscheles had arranged lodgings for him at 103 Great Portland Street. With Moscheles' help, letters of introduction and the fame of his grandfather, everyone who came into contact with Felix seems from the start to have been captivated by his personality. Even the German iron merchant, with whom he stayed at Great Portland Street, fell under the spell of this dashing, Byronic-figure with the quiet voice and fine clothes.

Musical and aristocratic circles were opened to him and, accompanied by Klingemann, he plunged into London's social whirl. Dancing, laughing, revelling in their second language and the absence of parental constraints, they were two young men-about-town, and enjoyed themselves enormously. Jokes and hoaxes followed. Someone claiming to be the Governor of Ceylon called on Felix to propose that he compose a festival anthem for the natives in honour of their emancipation. Felix, greatly amused, began signing his letters, 'Composer to the Island of Ceylon'.

After three days' merry hedonism, Felix wrote home that he could not begin to 'compress into a single letter what I've experienced in the last three days':

I hardly remember the chief events. Things toss and whirl about me as if I were in a vortex, and I'm whirled along with them. Not in the last six months in Berlin have I seen so many contrasts and such variety as in these last three days. Just turn to the right from my lodgings, walk down Regent Street and see the wide, bright thoroughfare with its arcades (alas! it's enveloped in thick fog again today) and the shops with signs as big as a man and the stage-coaches piled up with men and women. See men carrying advertising signs on which the graceful achievements of trained cats are proclaimed. See the beggars and the negroes and those fat John Bulls with their slender, beautiful daughters hanging on their arms. Ah, those daughters! However, don't be alarmed, there's no danger from that quarter, neither in Hyde Park, so densely populated with girls where I drove yesterday with Mme Moscheles (as the fashion demands), nor at the concerts, nor at the Opera (for I've already been to all those places)...

If you could see me beside the heavenly grand piano — which Clementis have sent me for the whole of my stay — by the cheerful fireside within my own four walls, with shoes and grey filigree stockings and olive-coloured gloves (for I'm going out to pay calls) and could you see the immense four-poster bed in the next room, in which at night I can walk to sleep, and the pretty curtains and old-fashioned furniture, my breakfast tea with dry toast still before me, the servant girl in curl-papers who has just brought me my newly-hemmed handkerchief, and asks for further orders, whereupon I attempt a polite English backward nod; and could you but see the highly respectable fog-enveloped street and hear the piteous voice with which a beggar down there now pours forth his ditty (he's almost drowned out by the street-vendors); and could you suspect that from here to the

*Felix had not long completed his overture *Calm Sea and Prosperous Voyage* based on a poem of Goethe's.

50

Hanover Square Rooms, where the Philharmonic Society performed in the 1840's. (British Museum).

city is a three-quarters-of-an-hour drive (and) that one has then traversed about a quarter of inhabited London, you might understand how it is that I'm half distracted.

Klingemann, Felix continued, hardly gave him time to recover from his sea-sickness before hauling him off to a coffee house where he read *The Times*. 'I looked first for the theatrical news. I saw that Rossini's *Otello* and the first appearance of Mme Malibran were announced for that very night':

In spite of weariness and sea-sickness, I resolved to go. Klingemann lent me the necessary grey stockings, as I couldn't find mine in a hurry, and yet had to appear in full dress, with a black cravat, like all the rest of the aristocracy. From there I went to the Italian Opera at King's Theatre where I got a seat in the pits (it cost me half a guinea). A large house, entirely decorated with crimson stuff, six tiers of boxes, out of which peep the ladies bedecked with great white feathers, and jewels of all kinds; an odour of pomade and perfume assails one on entering, and gave me a headache; in the pits, all the gentlemen, with fresh-trimmed whiskers; the house crowded; the orchestra quite good, conducted by Herr Spagnoletti (in December I'll give you an imitation of him; he's enough to make you die of laughter).

Maria Felicia Garcia (1808-36), known by first married name of Malibran. Operatic contralto.

As for Malibran, Felix was evidently attracted, but found her less enticing as a singer:

Malibran is a young woman, beautiful, with a gorgeous figure, full of fire and power, and at the same time coquettish; setting off her performance partly with clever embellishments of her own invention, partly with imitations of Pasta. She acts beautifully, her movements are convincing, but it's unfortunate that she so often exaggerates; something that borders on the ridiculous and disagreeable. . .

After the second act came a long divertissement with gymnastics and absurdities, just as with us at home, that went on till half past eleven. I was half dead with weariness, but held out till a quarter to one, when Malibran was dispatched, gasping and screaming disgustedly. That was enough and I went home.

The Italian Opera House
or King's Theatre in the
Haymarket, London.
(Mary Evans Library).

In the same letter, Felix gives a touching picture of Moscheles'
kindness and concern for his young friend. Throughout *Otello*,
Felix suffered occasional twinges of sea-sickness. 'I had constantly
to keep a firm hold on my seat', he wrote, 'because I still felt as if
the whole house was swaying to and fro':

On the day after, when I was still fast asleep, a hand touched me very gently, and
that could be nobody but Moscheles, who sat at my bed for a good hour, and
immediately gave me all kinds of advice. I can find no adequate expression for the
way Moscheles and his wife behave toward me. Whatever could possibly be agree-
able, useful, or advantageous to me, they have procured for me.

Still very much with Felix's first impressions of London, is an
amusing account of a visit to a display of 'Dr. Spurzheim's Cab-
inet', an exhibition extolling the validity of the latest quack science,
phrenology:

A group of murderers placed in contrast to a group of musicians interested me
greatly, and my belief in physiognomy received strong confirmation; really the
difference between Gluck's forehead and that of a parricide is striking. A beautiful
young English girl who was there desired to know whether she had a propensity
for stealing, or other crimes. As the aforesaid young lady had to undo her long hair
to allow the doctor to feel her bumps, and looked very beautiful with her hair
loose and when doing it up again before the mirror, I gave three cheers for
phrenology.

Mendelssohn as he would
have looked on his first
visit to London.

52

Accustomed to the plainer virtues of Biedermeier Berlin, Felix was dazzled by the opulence of Georgian London. He had his portrait painted by the fashionable artist of the moment, James Warren Childe, and with his grey frock coat, cravats, walking-cane, and top hat he looks every inch the dandy. He writes of a ball at the Duke of Devonshire's, and how the sumptuousness of the house seemed to him to spring from an oriental fairy tale; how the carriages choked the traffic in Piccadilly; how he saw, as he ascended the stairs, that the two men behind him were none other than Wellington and Peel.

He reports on the way the rooms were lit, with all the candelabras hidden by wreaths of red roses. He marvelled at the paintings; a life-size portrait by Van Dyck in one corner, a Titian in another, the walls covered with Correggios, Leonardos and works by the Flemish school. Young girls danced, couples flowing into an adjacent conservatory, opened to spread the scent of flowers through the house. The buffets, he wrote, were spread with 'the fruits of all seasons'. The young beaux flirted and waltzed 'excruciatingly', the older men lounged on divans, engaged in conversation with the ladies.

Save for a minor skirmish with his father over his decision not to use the approved 'Bartholdy', the first stage of Felix's Grand Tour progressed through a cloudless sky. Like Klingemann, he went to the theatre as often as he could, though was disappointed sadly by Kemble's Hamlet.

Top:
Charles Kemble (1775-1854). Manager of Theatre Royal, Covent Garden.

Top:
Fanny Horsley.

Bottom:
Sophy Horsley.

Drawings by
John Horsley.

Bottom left:
Devonshire House,
c. 1800.
(Mansell).

He thought it especially bad taste that Kemble (a friend of Smart's and, in fairness, more adept at lighter parts) appeared with one yellow and one black trouser leg to indicate madness. As a keen Shakespearean he was astonished also that cuts were made, and that Hamlet behaved throughout like a lunatic the King ought to have executed at once. The end, it seems, was especially novel:

When Hamlet expires with the words 'The Rest is Silence', Horatio let him lay there, proceeded to the footlights, and said 'Ladies and Gentlemen, tomorrow evening, *The Devil's Elixir'.' Thus ended *Hamlet* in England.

Felix also developed quickly a taste for English cookery, redolent descriptions being mailed home of plum pudding, cherry pie and 'german sausages' that one could purchase from street vendors and consume, *en route.*

Among the British musicians Felix met was Sir Thomas Attwood, a church composer and former pupil of Mozart. By then sixty-four, Attwood was still an outstanding organist at St. Paul's Cathedral.

A composer of glees, Dr. William Horsley introduced Mendelssohn to the English glee-club style. More importantly, he, his wife and daughters, Sophy and Fanny, became close friends, and Felix a welcome, if occasionally breathless, guest at their home amid the fields of Kensington.*

He seems to have let his hair down more easily with the Horsleys than in more elevated company. The sisters' book of reminiscences is as a result full of perceptive glimpses that give some idea of his energy and his restlessness. They recorded that, on a later visit:

Felix was very lachrymose and rushed four times in and out of the room in a very phrensied manner. I gazed at him for some time in such deep amaze that I am sure he at last perceived it. What an odd-tempered creature he is. Mama and Mary think Mendelssohn will never marry. I do, that is if he does not plague his mistress to death before the day arrives. He was dressed very badly and looked in want of the piece of soap and nailbrush which I have so often threatened to offer him.

Yet for all the warmth and friendliness of the welcome, Felix did not at first find it so easy to make his mark in the musical life of the capital. As a composer he was unknown, as a performer untried, the season already well advanced, and the remaining programmes agreed.

Wishing to show his worth as a composer rather than a virtuoso, he applied to the Philharmonic Society. They took their time in replying and in the event he did not make his début until 25 May, a month and more after his arrival. Felix blamed Sir George Smart for the delay, and in his letters home complained that Smart had brushed him aside with excuses. Later he went so far as to denounce him as an 'intriguing deceitful, and untruthful man'. More likely, Felix, became impatient and lost his temper.

*The Horsleys lived at 1 High Row, a large Georgian house not far from the present Notting Hill Gate station.

Henriette Sontag
Countess Rossi (1803-54).
Berlin *Prima Donna* and
rival to Malibran.

At any event, matters were arranged eventually and on 25 May
his first Symphony (save for the *minuet,* which was replaced for the
occasion by an orchestral version of the *scherzo* from the Octet) was
given at the seventh concert of the Philharmonic season. The day
after, Felix wrote home that:

When I came to the rehearsal of the symphony in the Argyll Rooms, I found the
whole orchestra assembled and about two hundred guests, mostly ladies, many of
them foreigners. First the Mozart Symphony in E flat was rehearsed, and mine
was to come next. I felt not precisely afraid but very keyed-up and excited. During
the Mozart rehearsal I took a little walk in Regent Street and looked at people.
When I came back everything was ready and they were waiting for me. I mounted
the podium, drew my little white baton from my pocket, one which I had made
specially for the purpose. The concertmaster, Cramer, showed me how the
orchestra was placed. Those at the back had to stand up so that I could see them, I
was introduced to all, greetings were exchanged. A little fellow with a stick
instead of a powdered and bewigged conductor caused a few laughs. We began.

Save for a few errors, the rehearsal went smoothly, and Mendelssohn reports that the orchestra liked it. 'After every movement the
people present applauded and so did the orchestra':

After the last movement they made a great to do. Again they broke out in
approval. The directors came to me. I had to go down to the audience and bow my
thanks right and left. I must have shaken two hundred hands. All those strangers
became acquaintances and friends within half an hour.

Happily, the concert itself was no less starry affair:

The success was greater than I could ever have dreamt. Cramer led me to the
piano as if I were a young girl and I was received with loud and long applause.
They wanted the adagio *da capo;* I preferred to indicate my thanks and go on, for
fear of boring the audience. But after the *scherzo* the demand for repetition was so
incessant that I had to play it again. At the end they applauded me as long as I
kept thanking the orchestra, and shook hands till I left the hall.

A few days later, he gave a recital, again in Argyll Rooms. Arriving
early to try the piano, he found it was locked. While a key was
being procured, he tried another 'grey with age' and fell to improvising, forgetting his surroundings until he realized that the
audience was already beginning to fill the hall, and that he had no
time to practise at the piano on which he was to perform.

Despite his anxiety and the heat (the auditorium was filled with
women in bright summer hats) the programme was well received.
Felix played, he felt, with particular abandon, noting that the hats
swayed in time to the music like a field of tulips. That the English
made an attentive audience for his playing was attested by Mendelssohn himself:

By God, I play better here than in Berlin, and that's because the people listen
better. Don't take that as conceit, but it is thrilling when you feel you succeed and
give others pleasure.

He played also Weber's tricky *Konzertstück* and several of his own
compositions, scoring a triumph with Beethoven's *Emperor*

Concerto which, to his audience's astonishment, he played from memory at a time when even Liszt thought it prudent to carry the score with him onto the platform. His fingers *sang*, wrote one critic. Another added, 'scarcely had he touched the keyboard than something that can only be described as similar to a pleasureable electric shock passed through his hearers and held them spell-bound'.

But his final acceptance came through a generous gesture. Out of the blue, his Uncle Nathan wrote asking help for the people of Silesia, recently laid waste by floods. Felix leapt into action, enlisting the help of soprano Henrietta Sontag, the current darling of London. Coup of coups, he then persuaded Malibran, Moscheles and others to join him in approaching the House of Lords, requesting *their* support.

Number 3, Chester Place, London. The home of the Moscheles. Drawing by Mendelssohn.

57

The whole affair, supervised by Felix, was engineered with remarkable skill — a further proof that when he wanted something, he would get it. The concert was sold out, with hundreds turned away at the doors and a few notables finally accommodated on stage among the double-basses. So many participants had been engaged that none could sing a solo aria, Felix combining them instead in ensembles. With Moscheles, he himself played his own Two-Piano Concerto, and conducted the *A Midsummer Night's Dream* Overture.

This was the concert, on 13 July, 1829, that finally established Felix as the darling of the British public. His relationship with England thereafter blossomed mutually into an affair of the heart. London he considered his second home, 'There is no question', he wrote from Naples a few months later, 'that "smokey nest" is my preferred city and will remain so. I feel quite emotional about it'. Even the press was happy. When he arrived, his presence had been little more than an item of gossip. *The Harmonicon's* 'Diary of a Dilettante' column gushed that he was 'the son of the rich banker of Berlin, and, I believe a grandson of the celebrated Jewish philosopher and elegant writer'. But on 22 July, *The Atheneum* could write:

A most extraordinary man, whose name we have not hitherto presented to our readers, and whose appearance here [at the Silesia concert] was one of the grand features of the concert. We allude to M. Mendelssohn, a piano-forte player of almost transcendent talent, which becomes more admirable when something of the man was known. He is very young, independent in station, his father being an opulent banker in Leipsic [*sic*]; and with a thirst and love of music nearly unparalleled, his modesty blinds him to the success with which he has cultivated it. He is now gone to the Irish lakes and it is expected that he will employ them as a subject for some future exercise of his skill in composition, [In this, *The Atheneum* was mistaken]. As a performer, his abilities are first-rate. In the act of playing he is lost to everything beside the instrument before him. His memory is represented as being the most wonderful of his faculties.

As Klingemann summed up, Felix on his first extended visit alone into the outside world, left behind him the impression of 'high talents and (of being) a perfect gentleman. A foreigner can hardly understand how much an Englishwoman includes in this expression':

It contains a whole volume of approbation. I imagine that Apollo himself could appear and play irresistibly on his lyre, but if as a liberty-loving Greek he were to decide not to drink wine with the mistress of the house, he would be landed with the definitive curse, 'He is no gentleman'. It is the severest curse of the civilised world.

Chapter 5

The Grand Tour

For nature then...
To me was all in all — I cannot paint
What then I was. The sounding cataract
Haunted me like a passion
       — WORDSWORTH

   ...a land
Which was the mightiest in its old
       command
And is the loveliest
Wherein were cast ... the men of
       Rome!

Thou art the garden of the world
       — BYRON

With the London season at an end, Mendelssohn was at last free to take a holiday. So, travelling by stage (fresh horses every ten miles, three stops a day for food), with Klingemann and a friend he made his way north to Edinburgh and the Scottish Highlands.

From a sophisticate's point of view, Scotland toward the beginning of the nineteenth century was a romantic place, full of mystery and wildness, its inhabitants strange, almost barbarian.

For an impressionable young man like Felix, the choice was a good one. Though they stayed only three days, he was much impressed with Edinburgh:

When God Himself takes to landscape-painting, it turns out strangely beautiful. Few of my Swiss reminiscences can compare to this; everything looks so stern and robust, half-enveloped in mist or smoke or fog; moreover there is to be a bagpipe competition tomorrow; many Highlanders came in costume from church, victoriously leading their sweethearts in their Sunday best and casting magnificent and important looks over the world; with long red beards, tartan plaids, bonnets and feathers, naked knees and their bagpipes in their hands, they passed quietly along by the half-ruined grey castle on the meadow, where Mary Stuart lived in splendour and saw Rizzio murdered. I feel as if time went at a very rapid pace when I have before me so much that was and so much that is.

View of Edinburgh,
c. 1834.

Very soon Felix formulated the idea of writing a 'Scottish' Symphony. On 30 July, he visited the ruined chapel of Mary Stuart at Holyrood House and there, in a moment, the seed was sown:

In the evening twilight we went today to the palace where Queen Mary lived and loved; a little room is shown there with a winding staircase leading up to the door; up this way they came and found Rizzio in that little room, pulled him out, and three rooms off there's a dark corner, where they murdered him. The chapel close to it is now roofless, grass and ivy grow there, and at that broken altar Mary was crowned Queen of Scotland. Everything round is broken and mouldering and the bright sky shines in. I believe I today found in that old chapel the beginning of my 'Scottish' Symphony.

Felix and Klingemann also visited Sir Walter Scott, author of the Waverley novels and, in George R. Marek's words, 'spokesman for derring-do and love in the glade'. Felix and Fanny had between them read almost every word of his historical romances (Goethe thought them some of the greatest books ever written), and it came as a disappointment that having at last made the pilgrimage to Scott's home at Abbotsford, the two friends found him indifferent to his admiring visitors.

Old, harassed and in domestic disarray, the great man was at his most unreceptive, faced by two young Germans with difficult accents and muddy boots. Felix wrote that all that resulted was 'a half hour of inconsequential conversation':

We found Sir Walter in the act of leaving Abbotsford, stared at him like fools, drove eighty miles and lost a day. Melrose compensated us but little; we were out of humour with great men, with ourselves, with the world, with everything. A bad day.

60

Like all good tourists, Mendelssohn and Klingemann were inveterate sightseers. The next four weeks they spent hunting out historic ruins and famous views. Felix's pencil was as active in his sketch pad as it was in composing prodigious letters home. Blessed with just as much exuberance, Klingemann also fired off a host of letters, and composed ditties to accompany his friend's drawings.

The size and silence of Scotland, its fogs, its wet pastures, its cliffs and waterfalls and its continuously billowing winds, all impressed Felix deeply. Even rough weather failed to damp his spirits:

This is a most dismal, melancholy, rainy day. But we continue as best we can, which in the circumstances isn't saying much. Earth and sky are wet through and whole regiments of clouds are still marching up. Yesterday was a lovely day, we passed from rock to rock, many waterfalls, beautiful valleys, with rivers, dark woods and heathland with the red heather in bloom...

[The Bridge of Tummel] is a wild affair! The storm howls, rushes and whistles, doors are banging and the window-shutters bursting open. There's no telling whether the watery noise is from the driving rain or the foaming stream as both rage together; we're sitting here quietly by the fire which I poke from time to time to make it flare up. The wet trickles down from one of the walls, the floor's so thin that conversation from the servant's room below penetrates up to us; they're singing drunken songs and laughing; dogs are barking.

We have beds with crimson curtains; on our feet, instead of English slippers, are Scotch wooden shoes; tea with honey and oat cakes. The servant girl came to meet us with whisky. It's very quiet and lonely here. The country, far and wide, is thickly overgrown with foliage, ample water is rushing under the bridge from all sides. There's little corn, much heather, precipices, passes, crossways, beautiful green everywhere, deep blue water everywhere — but all stern, dark, very lonely...

I've invented a new method of drawing (because of the weather) and have rubbed in clouds today and painted grey mountains with my pencil. Klingemann is rhyming briskly, and I finish my sketches during the rain.

View of the Trossachs.
Drawing by Mendelssohn.

61

View of Killiecrankie in
Blair Atholl. Drawing by
Mendelssohn.

From a letter of Klingemann's, dated 7 August, we learn that Felix
and he made their way to Tobermory by way of Fort William and
Oban, where they rested in preparation for their trip the following
day to the islands of Staffa and Iona:

Yesterday we went up hill and down dale, our cart generally rolling on without us,
we ourselves stalking through the heather, under clouds, and in a thick drizzling
rain. Smoky huts were stuck on cliffs, ugly women looked through the window-
holes, cattle-herds with Rob Roys now and then blocked the way. Late last night
we unexpectedly stumbled on a bit of culture again, viz. the one street of which
Fort William consists, and this morning we embraced the very newest piece of
culture, steam, and were again among many people, greedily enjoying sunshine
and the sea. Good cheer and society of all kinds.

A new friend told us that yonder young couple were on their honeymoon, and
that he had seen them on Ben Lomond, shortly after the wedding, dance the
Scotch reel, the bride with tears in her eyes.

Sight of Staffa the next day was to prove especially fruitful, the
black basalt cavern of Fingal's Cave so impressing Felix that he
sketched out straight away (in the course of a letter to Fanny), the
opening theme of what was to become the *Hebrides* Overture. As
Hiller later recalled:

Mendelssohn had brought with him to Paris the draft score of the *Hebrides*
Overture. He told me that not only was its general form and colour suggested to
him by the sight of Fingal's Cave, but that the first few bars, containing the
principal subject, had actually occurred to him on the spot. The same evening he
and his friend Klingemann paid a visit to a Scotch family. There was a piano in
the drawing-room, but being Sunday, music was utterly out of the question, and
Mendelssohn had to employ all his diplomacy to get the instrument opened for a
single moment, so that he and Klingemann might hear the theme which forms the
germ of that original and masterly overture.

Top: Fingal's Cave.
Inspiration for
Mendelssohn's *Hebrides*
Overture. Wood
engraving, c. 1850.
(George Rainbird Ltd)

Opening bars of the
Hebrides Overture
contained in a letter
written by Mendelssohn
to his sister, Fanny,
18.2.1829.

Felix, though, cannot have altogether enjoyed seeing Fingal's Cave.*

Once again he succumbed violently to sea-sickness, while what Hiller referred to as 'the germ' of the overture was to undergo numerous revisions before finding its final form.

A model of clarity and delicate orchestration, the finished result impressed even Wagner as being 'an aquarelle by a great scene painter', and from the music that floated into Mendelssohn's mind out of the wind and waves of the Atlantic it is clear that what for Klingemann was no more than a 'monstrous organ, black, resounding and utterly with purpose' had stirred Felix far more deeply. As deeply, in fact, as it had the poet Keats who, ten years earlier on a visit to that wild, stony island, had written:

Suppose, now, the giants who came down to the daughters of men had taken a whole mass of these columns and bound them together like bunches of matches, and then with immense axes had made a cavern in the body of these columns. Such is Fingal's cave, except that the sea has done the work of excavation and is continually dashing there. The colour of the columns is a sort of black, with a lurking gloom of purple therein. For solemnity and grandeur it far surpasses the finest cathedral.

Thereafter, the two friends travelled south, through Glasgow and the Lake District, to Liverpool. Klingemann thence returned to London, while Felix, having chanced his arm on the newly-opened railway that ran through the Mersey Tunnel, headed for Wales. His first recorded impressions of that country are of its folk music, a raucous affair his urbane temperament found painful. From an inn at Llangollen he wrote:

No national music for me! Ten thousand devils take all nationality! Now I am in Wales and, dear me, a harper sits in the hall of every reputed inn, playing incessantly so-called national melodies; that is to say, most infamous, vulgar, out-of-tune trash, with a hurdygurdy going on at the same time. It's maddening, and has given me a toothache already. Scotch bagpipes, Swiss cow-horns, Welsh harps, all playing the Huntsman's Chorus with hideously improvised variations — then their beautiful singing in the hall — altogether their music is beyond conception.

His destination was Coed du, near Chester, and a well-to-do family, the Taylors, to whom he had an introduction. When he arrived, he settled very happily, though not before writing home complaining once more about the weather that seems to have dogged his every step. 'Yesterday', he wrote ironically, 'was a good day — that means I was only soaked through three times. I had to wear my coat continuously but once or twice got a glimpse of the sun through the clouds'.

The attraction of Coed du was evidently the Taylor girls, all dressed in white and disposed to make a great fuss of their handsome visitor. Mr Taylor, a prosperous mine-owner, seems to have

* The name comes from the Gaelic *Fionn na Ghal*, Chief of Valour.

possessed a fine piano, on which Felix willingly played any number of his own compositions and a few songs by Fanny.

For the three sisters — Susan, Honoria and Anne — he wrote his three *Fantasias or Caprices*, the first being suggested by a bunch of carnations and roses, the second by some small trumpet-like flowers that one of the girls wore in her hair, the third by a stream. The daughters in turn observed closely the charming stranger with the flashing eyes and coal-black locks:

Soon we began to find a most accomplished mind had come among us, quick to observe, delicate to distinguish. There was a little shyness about him, great modesty. We knew little about his music, but the wonder of it grew upon us; and I remember one night when my two sisters went to our rooms how we began saying to each other 'Surely this must be a man of genius...'.

We observed how natural objects seemed to suggest music to him. There was in my sister Honoria's garden, a pretty creeping plant, new at the time, covered with little trumpet-like flowers. He was struck with it, and played for her the music which (he said) the fairies might play on those trumpets. When he wrote out the piece (called *Capriccio in E minor*) he drew a little branch of that flower all up the margin of the page.

He was so far from any sort of pretension, or from making a favour of giving his music to us, that one evening when the family from a neighbouring house came to dinner, and we had dancing afterwards, he took his turn in playing quadrilles and waltzes with the others. He was the first person who taught us gallopades.

Such did Felix pass the summer of 1829. Yet by the end of August the prospect of returning home was becoming attractive. For one thing, Felix wanted to be back in Berlin in time for Fanny's wedding in October. The plan was to meet his father in Holland, the two returning to celebrate both the wedding and, shortly afterwards, Abraham and Lea's silver wedding anniversary.

Sketch appended to a joint letter from Mendelssohn, Moscheles and Chorley on their arrival at Ostend.

65

An unpleasant accident intervened however, when Felix — full of ideas for his E flat String Quartet, Op 12 and an organ piece for Fanny's wedding — was thrown from a carriage, badly damaging his knee.

He was aggrieved especially that convalescence would cause him to be parted from his sister on her wedding day. A week after the accident, he wrote Fanny an emotional letter:

This then is the last letter you'll receive before your marriage. For the last time I address you as Fräulein Fanny Mendelssohn-Bartholdy.

There's much I would like to say to you. But I'm not really able to. True, since yesterday I'm allowed to sit up a little every day and therefore it's easier for me to write. But my head is still completely confused from all that lying around in bed and from that long period of thinking nothing.

I feel as if I had lost the reins with which formerly I was able to guide my life. When I think about everything which is now going to change, and take a different shape, everything which I have long taken for granted, then my thoughts become unclear and half wild. I'm unable to organise them.

Well, live and prosper, marry and be happy, build your life in such a way that I'll find it beautiful and comfortable when I come to visit you (and that will be very soon), and stay the same as you were. Outside let the wind blow. I know both of you and that's sufficient. Whether I call my sister Fräulein or Madam is unimportant. The name is unimportant.

As Felix recovered, he noticed how quickly time passed. English friends visited him continuously, showering him with gifts of fruit, sweets, books, and flowers, while the faithful Klingemann was with Felix every moment he could spare from his diplomatic work. As Felix wrote, 'I shall never be able to thank him enough. Soon it's dusk again and the fat serving girl appears with my dinner. Soon the little night light will be burning next to my bed. I lie here and peer out and see when the day will break once more.'

After almost two months (during which he cultivated a luxurious set of sidewhiskers), he was allowed to take a short ride, and was so overcome at seeing the sun again that he wrote his father an effusive letter thanking him for all his love and admitting that when he was not daydreaming he had his nose buried in eighteenth-century literature. A long pipe and a night cap, he said and he could easily be mistaken for a gout-ridden old uncle.

At the same time, he stayed a few days with Attwood, uncovering at Attwood's home in Norwood, a full score of Weber's *Euryanthe*. From this, Felix had the great satisfaction of confirming that he had guessed correctly about the scoring of a certain passage. Disappointed though he may have been at missing Fanny's wedding, Felix wrote with unstinting appreciation of the kindness of his friends in England. His last fortnight in London, he described as 'the happiest and richest I have spent there'.

He arrived home in good time for his parent's silver wedding celebrations on 26 December. For days previous, the younger members of the family and their friends had rehearsed secretly in the garden house Felix's little singspiel *Son and Stranger,* an en-

Overture to
Mendelssohn's Operetta
Son and Stranger,
composed in 1829 for
Mendelssohn's parents'
silver wedding.

gaging piece with a libretto by Klingemann that tells of the various
misunderstandings and complications that arise when the long-lost
son returns to test his bride's faithfulness. For one song, composer
and librettist changed places, Felix writing the words and Klingemann the music. The part of Schulz was specially written for Wilhelm Hensel. Knowing his brother-in-law to be tone deaf, Felix
wrote the part on one note only. Even this it seems, proved too
difficult — Devrient records that at the first performance Hensel
failed to find it, despite the fact that 'it was blown and whistled him
on every side'.

The principal role was assigned to Devrient, and everything was going to plan when the Crown Prince at the last moment ordered a Court concert, commanding Devrient to appear on the very evening scheduled for *Son and Stranger*.

When Felix was told, he fell into an extraordinary state, becoming hysterical and babbling incoherently in English. The doctor having hastily been summoned, he sent Felix to bed, where he slept soundly for twelve hours. When he awoke from this curious lapse, he appeared quite normal and to have no memory of it.

In the meantime, Abraham had pulled strings at court, and gained a special dispensation for Devrient to appear first on the bill for the Crown Prince, before dashing across to 3 Leipzigerstrasse. *Son and Stranger* proved in the event a great success, but Felix was, as usual, dissatisfied and refused to countenance its publication.

About now, Mendelssohn started work in earnest on a more serious project, the *Reformation* Symphony, which he intended for the tercentenary of the Augsburg Protestant Confession. At the time, there were in the Mendelssohn family circle frequent arguments about the political situation in France. Felix's views, according to Devrient, seeming almost revolutionary to his conservative father and brother-in-law.

Further aggravation may have come from the fact that in 1830 the University of Berlin founded a new professorship of music. It was hoped that Felix might take this, but he declined, feeling perhaps he was too highly strung and volatile to be a really good teacher.

He was, besides, keen to embark on further adventures, more especially to travel south, like so many of his countrymen, to the land of blue skies and clear seas, 'where the lemon trees bloom'. His father's consent having at last been obtained, an attack of measles delayed his plans, and only in May, 1830 did he set out on the first stage of a journey that was to keep him on the move for the best part of the next three years.

As far as Dessau, Felix was accompanied by his father. There he stayed for a time with his friend Schubring. From Dessau, Felix went alone to Weimar, to greet for the last time the man who, in his youth, had been inspired to the heights by contemplation of classical antiquity. Goethe by now was ageing fast, and Felix described him as 'an old lion who wants to go to sleep'. Felix played him some of his piano works, including the F sharp minor *Fantasy* and the three pieces he had written in Wales.

He played also Beethoven's Fifth Symphony, rather to Goethe's distaste. 'That', the old man said, 'causes no emotion. It's merely strange and grandiose'. Mendelssohn's portrait was painted while he stayed with Goethe, and he sent Fanny his newly completed Symphony, canvassing advice over its title:

Try to collect opinions as to the title I ought to select: 'Reformation' Symphony, 'Confession' Symphony, Symphony for a Church Festival, 'Juvenile' Symphony or whatever you like. Write me about it and instead of all the stupid suggestions, send me one clever one; but I also want to hear all the nonsensical ones that are sure to be produced.

For all its warmth, there are, once or twice, hints that Mendelssohn's friendship with Goethe was more strained than hitherto. Trying to interest Felix in science and natural history, Goethe argued that no one should be content with a 'one-sided mentality'. When Felix appeared to rebuff the implied criticism, the older man angrily turned his back on him. At the time, Felix was sitting at the piano and, as if to comfort himself, began to improvise; whereupon Goethe re-entered the room and said simply, 'You have enough. Hold fast to what you have'.

In the end, Goethe was more than usually reluctant to let Felix go:

Then the old man himself entered and said, 'What's all this about your leaving in a hurry?'. He had still lots to tell me and I had a lot to play for him. As to my journey's goal, that was unimportant.

But Felix at last insisted on leaving, and Goethe gave him as a parting gift a page of the *Faust* manuscript with the inscription, 'To my dear young friend, Felix Mendelssohn, that strong but sensitive master of the piano, in happy memory of great May days, 1830'.

From Weimar, Felix made his way to Munich. Marx, who met him there, wrote Fanny a glowing account of his great social success. Once more, Felix seems to have captivated a goodly number of musicians. He also found time to poke fun at the court and to attend a bad performance of *Fidelio*, of which he wrote:

Isn't Germany a crazy place? It brings forth great men and then doesn't honour them. It produces quantities of great singers, many fine artists, but none who play a part simply and unaffectedly. Marcellina tears her role to tatters, Jacquino is a simpleton, the Minister a sheep. If a German like Beethoven writes an opera, a German like a Stuntz or Poissl (or whoever) cuts the *ritornelli* and similar 'unimportant' passages while another adds trombones to the symphonies. A third then states that B[eethoven] over-orchestrated.

Felix also became involved in Munich with a beautiful young pianist, the sixteen-year old Delphine von Schauroth, for whom he composed his G minor Piano Concerto. Years later, he confided to Schumann that Delphine could have become 'dangerous' to him. They played duets together, flirted, and Felix was strongly attracted to a young woman as intelligent as she was alluring. To Fanny, he wrote 'When the other day we played duets for the first time, she made an extraordinary impression on me'. Later we find Felix writing to his sister: 'I run day after day to the museum and twice a week to Schauroth, where I hang around a long time. We flirt outrageously but it isn't dangerous because I'm already in love with someone else — a Scotch girl whose name I don't know'.

At the time, Fanny was expecting her first child. On 14 June, Felix sent her from Vienna a *Song Without Words*, and a fortnight later, another to celebrate the birth of a boy (this is the spirited piece in B minor that appeared later, slightly revised, as No.2 of Opus 30).

For the next eight weeks, Felix toured in succession Salzburg, Linz, and Vienna, thence to Budapest, in time to witness the crowning of King Ferdinand V of Hungary. At last, on 10 October, he arrived in Venice, in time to find autumn brushing with gold that strange and beautiful city of water. Like many another visitor, Felix was entranced. 'Italy at last', he wrote. 'And what I have all my life considered as the greatest possible felicity is now begun, and I am basking in it'. Among his first acts was to write the haunting *Gondola Song,* Op 19 No. 6. This he did to 'to escape the town band playing in St. Mark's Square'.

What caught him most about Venice (indeed, all Italy) was the churches and their fabulous bounty. Titian's *Entombment and Ascension* led him to write that:

I knew (Titian) had enjoyed life and the good things of life, but he must have known as well the deepest sorrow. Equally, though, he must have known what it is to be in heaven. Maria floats on a cloud and the air stirs through the whole picture. One feels her breath, her unease and yet her devotion. A thousand emotions all in one painting! And what words can one use which don't sound banal and dry, compared to what the painting conveys?

Of the music he heard, though, he was critical. To Zelter he wrote indignantly that:

As I was earnestly contemplating the delightful evening landscape with its trees, and angels among the boughs, the organ commenced. The sound was at first quite in harmony with my feelings: but the second, third, and in fact all the rest, quickly roused me from my reveries and sent me straight home, for the man was playing in church, and during divine service, and in front of respectable people thus: [here Mendelssohn quotes a trite tune in common time] with the *Martyrdom of St. Peter* actually close beside him.

As on his French travels five years before, he was shocked by the general ignorance of music:

Not one of the best pianoforte players there, male or female, ever played a note of Beethoven, and when I hinted that he and Mozart were not to be despised, they said: 'So you are an admirer of classical music?' — 'Yes', said I.

From Venice he journeyed to Bologna, then to Florence, marvelling — like every fugitive from northern climes — at the bright translucent skies, the crystalline air and the wealth of flowers in bloom. But again it was the painting and the statues that drew his most ardent enthusiasm. Of Raphael's *Madonna del Cardellino* and the Venus of Medici he wrote with particular fervour.

Less happy were his dealings with innkeepers and coachmen, who he condemned wholesale as 'disgusting crooks ... finally I became dizzy with all the cheating. I no longer knew to whom they were lying, so whatever they said, I'd protest and declare "I'm not going to pay"'... that made things tolerable'.

The Spanish Steps.
The house of
Mendelssohn's uncle,
Jakob Bartholdy, is on the
right of the picture.
(Bodleian).

A week later, he threw over Florence for Rome, arriving shortly after dawn on 1 November, 'in bright and shining moonlight', with the sky 'a deep blue'. He then proceeded to find lodgings and settle for the winter, seeing the sights, composing, and making many friends and acquaintances. A few days after arriving, he described his daily regime:

Picture a small, two-windowed house on the Spanish Steps. In my room on the first floor there's a good Viennese piano. On the table lie portraits of Palestrina, Allegri etc., with their scores and Latin psalm book, from which one can compose a *non nobis*. This is where I live.

When in the morning I come into this room and the sun sparkles brightly on my breakfast (in me a poet was lost), I feel wonderful. Is it not late fall? And who at home would dare ask for warm, clear skies, grapes or flowers? After breakfast I set to work, I play and sing and compose until midday. After that the whole immeasurable Rome lies before me like some exercise in enjoyment. I do it very slowly, choosing every day something different, something of historic interest. One day I go walking among the antique ruins of the city, another to the Galleria Borghese or the Capitol of St. Peter's or the Vatican. That's how every day becomes unforgettable, and because I take my time every impression remains firm and indelible. When I'm working in the morning I don't want to stop ... then I say to myself 'You must see the Vatican'. Then when I'm there, I don't want to leave. Every occupation gives me pure pleasure and one enjoyment follows another. Venice with its past seemed to me a gravestone, those crumbling modern palaces and the continuous reminders of a former splendour put me out of sorts and saddened me. Rome's past seems to me like history itself. Its monuments inspire whether they make one feel serious or gay. It's satisfying to think that human beings can accomplish something which continues to refresh and strengthen them even after a thousand years.

As luck would have it, Felix had the good fortune to be in Rome at an eventful time. Though political disturbances were to cut short the festival, he took part in the Roman Carnival with its bright lights and gaiety. During his stay, Pope Pius VIII died, and he was able to watch not only the lavish Papal funeral, but also to wait on the conclave that followed, hear the cannonfire that signalled the election of the new Pope, and watch the official enthronement of Gregory XVI (Felix commented caustically on the casual attitude of the Italians, whose one anxiety was that Pius might be tactless enough to die in February and so upset the Carnival festivities). In a document that confirms his sharp ear and excellent memory, he sent Zelter a detailed abstract of the music heard during Holy Week.

Meanwhile, at home Abraham Mendelssohn had become increasingly difficult and irritable. Felix, who in the past had had differences with his father about the music of Beethoven and knew how to handle him, wrote to his brothers and sisters urging them to be tactful towards their father. To Abraham, he wrote a long and affectionate birthday letter, enclosing the opening bars of an unfinished piano piece.

Eager to make friends, Felix soon found himself well received by Roman society and the sizeable colony of expatriate Germans. Particular favourites were Baron Bunsen, Prussian Minister to Rome, and the Duke of Torlonia, whose family profession as banker had already brought him into contact with the Mendelssohns.

In the artistic community he was on good terms with the painter Horace Vernet, director of the French Academy at the Villa Medici, and Thorvaldson, the sculptor. Mendelssohn seems frequently to have played for Vernet while the painter worked away at his easel. He had wit enough, on the other hand, to see through the pretension of the would-be artists and *poseurs* who, day in, day out, lounged around the street cafes. 'Really horrible people', for example:

... sit around in the Café Greco. Still standing, on Via Condolti. I hardly ever go there, because they and their hangout make me suffer. They wear great broad hats, mongrel dogs crouch beside them, and their face, neck, and cheeks are entirely covered with hair. They puff up a terrible cloud of smoke, hurl insults at one another. The dogs see to it that the fleas are spread around. A tie or a decent coat would be a novelty. Whatever the beard doesn't cover the eyeglasses hide. So they drink coffee and prattle of Titian and Pordenone as if those two sat next to them and also wore beards and storm hats. And what they paint are sickly madonnas, weak-kneed saints, milksops of heroes. One feels like kicking them. If I never accomplish anything in my life, the least I'll do is show my contempt to those who have no respect for genius.

Everywhere he went, he was shocked by the lack of first-class music. In later years, he quipped that the best Italian singers came from anywhere bar Italy. The Vatican Chorus, in particular, was a tired group of voices who failed to sing even traditional pieces correctly. The orchestras he pronounced 'beneath contempt'. Few knew anything about music. In Venice, a customs official had confiscated his manuscripts, suspecting they contained a secret code.

Yet the natural beauty of the country so excited Felix that he

St Peters Cathedral, Rome
(Mary Evans Library)

composed with a will. Come December 1830, and the first version
of the *Hebrides* Overture was complete. The previous month he had
finished his setting of *Psalm CXV*, the *Scottish* and *Italian*
Symphonies both proceeded apace while, early in 1831, he began his
cantata after Goethe's *The First Walpurgis Night*.

As he explained to Zelter, he drew inspiration from anything save
Italian music. Nature was a particular stimulant. 'The sea lay
between the islands, and the rocks, covered with vegetation bent
over it then just as they do now. These are the antiquities that
interest me and are much more suggestive than crumbling
masonry'. Besides, why complain about the music when much else
was in no less sorry a state?

If one sees that a part of the loggias of Raphael are scratched out with unspeakable
crudeness and unimaginable barbarism in order to make way for inscriptions
scrawled in pencil, when one sees that the beginnings of the rising arabesques are
altogether ruined because the Italians destroy them with their knives or God
knows how, just to incise their miserable names, when one sees that somebody
wrote in large letters and with great emphasis 'Christ!' right underneath the
Apollo Belvedere, when one sees that in the centre of Michelangelo's *Last Judgement* an altar is erected large enough to cover the whole middle of the picture and
thus disturb and ruin the whole effect, when one observes that through the
magnificent rooms of the Villa Madama, where Giulio Romano painted his

frescoes, the cattle are driven and cabbages stored merely out of indifference to the beautiful — so that is all much worse than having terrible orchestras, and it ought to pain painters more than second-rate music pains me. The people are at the same time involved and silly. They have a religion but don't believe in it; they have a Pope and clerics but mimic them; they have a brilliant past and quite remove themselves from it. No wonder that art means little to them — they take the sublime so indifferently.

As spring 1831 came on, Felix ventured further afield, to Naples and the islands of Ischia and Capri. A project for visiting Sicily, though, was discouraged by his father. Travelling light — 'three shirts and Goethe's poems' — he sent home meticulous descriptions of all he saw.

Naples seemed to him on the surface a 'merry place', but beneath the glitter he was not slow to find a 'mass of misery':

I'm pained by the incredible mass of beggars who haunt one at every step and surround one's carriage as soon as it stops; above all the white-haired old people one sees. Such a mass of misery is difficult to picture. If I go walking along the street and look at the ocean and islands, there's no problem. But when I turn round I find that I'm standing in the midst of cripples or as happened to me recently I'm surrounded by thirty or forty children shouting *'Muio di fame'* and knocking their cheeks to show they have nothing to chew on!

In Naples, Felix also renewed contact with Julius Benedict, the latter marvelling at Mendelssohn's piano playing at a party. 'Without a moment's hesitation', Benedict wrote, 'he introduced first one theme of the pieces just performed, then another, added a third and a fourth, and worked them simultaneously in the most brilliant way'.

Eventually, with May drifting into June and the Italian spring slipping into high summer, Felix retraced his steps to Florence. En route, he had a trying encounter with a coach driver, writing to his sisters that:

... he doesn't allow you to sleep and lets you starve and thirst. In the evenings when he ought to allow time for supper he drives in such a way that one arrives toward midnight, when everybody's asleep and one must be grateful to find a bed. In the morning he departs at 3.15. At midday he stops his five hours, choosing without fail the one inn where there's nothing to eat. He drives his six German miles a day and drives *piano* while the sun shines *fortissimo*. I was particularly unlucky, my travelling companions being quite unsympathetic, inside three Jesuits and outside, where I preferred to sit, an unpleasant Venetian woman. If I wanted to escape her, I had to listen to unstinting praise of Charles X and how Ariosto should really have been burned as a seducer and despoiler. Outside it was worse still and the carriage made no progress. The first day, after a journey of four hours, the axle broke and we had to stop for nine hours in front of a country house where we happened to be. Finally we were forced to spend the night there. In Incisa half a day's journey from Florence, I couldn't stand the carriage driver's rudeness and insults a moment longer. I just unloaded my things and told him to drive to the devil, advice he didn't appreciate.

After a comical episode involving a lady innkeeper and the local police chief, Felix eventually procured from an elderly vintner a small carriage in which he sped the last leg to Florence and the annual St. John's Day Festival:

Off we went across the mountains toward Florence. After half an hour we passed the stage coach. My umbrella protected me from the sun. Indeed, I've seldom travelled as pleasantly and amusingly, my troubles behind me and the prospect of a fine festival before me.

Having plunged into the fairground atmosphere, visited a masked ball that lasted until one in the morning, and watched a procession of brightly-lit barges on the Arno, Felix again chose to spend his time haunting the Florentine museums. 'Today I spent the whole morning from ten to three in the Uffizi gallery,' he wrote, 'It was heavenly'. Raphael's self-portrait seemed to him:

... almost the most touching picture of his I've seen. In the middle of a tall wall, covered with portraits, hangs a smallish and not especially famous painting. My eyes went to it at once: Raphael — young, very ill, pale, longing to go on, mouth and eyes filled with desire and longing. It was as if I could gaze into his soul. He can't yet express all he sees and feels. How something forces him to persevere and how he must die an early death — that's expressed in that fierce, suffering face. As you look into those dark eyes with their gaze springing from the depths or at the lips drawn in pain, you almost shudder.

Yet in spite of these many and varied distractions, in spite of the hours spent sitting in his favourite armchair and drinking in Titians, Peruginos and Raphaels, he kept on working steadily at his music. At the same time as Felix was rhapsodizing over the Uffizi, he was hard at work on the *Italian* Symphony.

In Venice, the first book of the *Songs Without Words* had been completed. He additionally kept up a steady output of church music, including psalm settings, motets, chorales, and the prayer *Verlieh und Frieden*.

Florence, with view of Duomo. Sketch by Mendelssohn.

75

Louis Hector Berlioz (1803-69). The greatest musical figure in the French romantic movement.

But while he had begun much, he had completed relatively little since the start of his travels. The facile youth was becoming a hesitant adult, working but slowly, polishing each bar, phrase and modulation like a diamond-cutter at work on priceless stones. Inspiration came quickly, but then followed the task of chipping away ideas until they were fine-honed into a pleasing whole. This, admittedly, seems not to have worried Felix. As he wrote Devrient:

I'm as unconcerned with fame as I am with obtaining the post of *Kapellmeister*. It would be nice if both happened. Yet as long as I don't starve to death it's my duty to work as my heart dictates. My only thought, ever present, is honestly to compose as I feel things and less and less because of outer considerations. If I've composed a piece and it's from my heart, I've absolved my duty. I don't care whether it brings fame, honours, distinctions or snuffboxes.

While in Rome, Felix met Berlioz. On the surface, one might think the romantic streak in Berlioz — the imagination that could give birth to the *Fantastic Symphony* and *Harold in Italy* — would have appealed to the man who had composed the overture to *A Midsummer Night's Dream*. But Mendelssohn's romanticism was of a different order, imbued with a classicism and rectitude far from the wild, opium-induced midnight visions of the disconcerting Frenchman, described by Théophile Gautier as an 'exasperated eagle'.

It was a meeting of chalk and cheese. Mendelssohn neither understood nor approved Berlioz' art, while his feelings about Berlioz' personality were, to say the least, equivocal. When they met, Berlioz was twenty-seven and, at his fourth attempt, had finally won the coveted *Prix de Rome*.* He was now a student at the Villa Medici, an excitable, eyeball-rolling character, bursting with ideas and usually infatuated with some girl or other.

By nature garrulous and unruly, Berlioz always declared his views with vehemence. As a composer, he allowed his inspiration similarly free rein, and was happy to juxtapose pages of sublime inspiration with others of mediocrity. No wonder the gentle Felix found him a prickly customer.

Despite the number of things they had in common — a love for Shakespeare, Goethe and Beethoven, a hatred for amateurism, great skill in orchestration — Mendelssohn could happily dismiss Berlioz as 'bent', throwing in for good measure that he considered the Frenchman to have 'not even a speck of talent', and that 'thinking himself the creator of new worlds' he merely continued 'to grope in the dark':

You say, mother dear, Berlioz ought to know what he wants artistically. I am not at all of your opinion. I thinks he wants to get married. I think he is worse than others because he is a *poseur*. I do not like his wild enthusiasm nor the way he makes a fool of himself over women, nor the black-and-white extremes of his genius. If he weren't a Frenchman, I couldn't stick him at all.

* With his cantata *Sardanopoulos*.

76

With tact and diplomacy, Felix did, however, keep his feelings well under wraps. As a result, Berlioz came to admire Mendelssohn the man as much as Mendelssohn the musician:

We get along very well. He's an admirable fellow and his executant talent is as great as his creative genius, which is saying a great deal. Everything I have heard by him delights me. I firmly believe that he is one of the highest musical talents of our epoch. It was he who acted as my guide [in Rome], and every morning when I called on him he would play me a Beethoven sonata, and together we would sing Gluck's *Armide*. Then he would take me to see the ruins which, however, impressed me little. Mendelssohn has one of those candid souls one comes across so rarely. He believes firmly in his Lutheran religion, and I used to scandalize him by poking fun at the Bible. He was responsible for the only tolerable moments which I enjoyed during my stay in Rome.

Berlioz later wrote to Hiller that, 'he has an enormous, extraordinary, superb and prodigious talent. I cannot be accused of flattering him in telling you this, because he told me frankly he did not understand my music at all'.

Felix once said that he felt like taking a good bite out of Berlioz, so irritated did he become by his apparently grotesque posturing. But then Hector would start eulogising Gluck or Beethoven, and Felix had no choice but warmly to agree with him.

As for Mendelssohn's knowledge of the Frenchman's music, Berlioz claimed in his *Memoirs* that 'at the time I had hardly produced anything. Mendelssohn knew only my *Irish Melodies* (and) the *King Lear* Overture which I had just composed in Nice'. Yet this contradicts a salty letter from Felix to his father, in which he tells of playing through at the piano with Berlioz, the *Fantastic Symphony:*

... which is called 'Episodes in the Life of an Artist' and for which a printed programme is passed round. In the 1st movement, the poor artist goes to the devil: somewhere the audience would love to have gone long before. All the instruments have a hangover and positively vomit notes. But he is a very pleasant fellow, speaks well and has fine ideas so you can't help but like him.

For all their differences, Mendelssohn came to hold for Berlioz a certain respect. He could still complain to Moscheles much later that Berlioz' orchestration was 'terribly dirty. One feels like washing one's hands after handling one of his scores'. But with time he came to regard Berlioz as something more than a *poseur*. When Berlioz, in 1843, expressed a wish to have his music played at the Leipzig *Gewandhaus* (where Mendelssohn was music director), Felix spared no effort to assist his old acquaintance.

Berlioz declared that Felix acted like a brother, hunting out strange instruments, correcting parts and, at the concert, playing on the piano the harp part, the harpist having gone missing.

Similarly, Berlioz conducted Mendelssohn's music with the greatest care, the critic of *The Times* writing in 1852 that Berlioz' account of the *Italian* Symphony was the finest in his experience, and one in which every tempo was perfectly gauged.

As the summer of 1831 drew on, Felix — in no hurry to return home — made his way northward. In Milan, he stayed a week and met the Ertmann family. The record he left forms an important part in the biographical literature on Beethoven, Dorothea Ertmann having been the friend and admirer (possibly more) of the great man (the inscription of the Opus 101 Piano Sonata reads to his 'dear and beloved Dorothea Caecila').

At two o'clock I presented myself to Freifrau Dorothea von Ertmann. She received me with great courtesy, and was most obliging, playing me Beethoven's C sharp minor and D minor sonatas. The Old General (Dorothea's husband) was quite enchanted and had tears in his eyes because it was so long since he had heard his wife play. She mentioned the trio in B flat [the *Archduke*] but said she could not remember it. I played it, and sang the other parts: this enchanted the old couple. She plays Beethoven's works admirably, though it's so long since she studied them she sometimes rather exaggerates, dwelling too long on one passage, then hurrying the next; but there are many parts she plays magnificently and I think I've learned something from her. When I was approaching the end of the adagio (in the Trio) she exclaimed, 'The expression here is beyond anyone's ability'; and it's quite true. The following day, when I want there again to play the C minor Symphony to her, she insisted on my taking my coat off, the day was so hot. She relates the most interesting anecdotes about Beethoven, and that when she was playing to him in the evenings he not infrequently used the candle snuffers as a toothpick!

At the same time, Felix also made the acquaintance of Karl Mozart, the elder of Mozart's two sons, a quiet, lonely little man employed as a menial figure at the Austrian legation. So delighted was he by Mendelssohn's playing of his father's music, that he gave him letters of introduction to a number of friends in Como.

While he was in Milan, Felix also had an illuminating correspondence with Devrient who had been urging his friend to try his hand at a full-scale opera. In his reply, Felix dwells on the problem of finding the right libretto. His slightly moralistic, Teutonic approach to music — so marked on his first trip to Paris — continued through his life, especially where opera was concerned. On a later occasion, he wrote from Paris criticizing rather priggishly the libretti for Auber's *Fra Diavolo* and Meyerbeer's *Robert le Diable*. Whatever libretto he chose, his frame of mind would probably have prevented him from being a musical dramatist of the calibre of a Mozart or a Verdi.

The next two months Felix passed in Switzerland, much time as usual being spent on foot. Highlights included strenuous excursions up and down the Jungfrau, the Rigi, the Frauhorn and the Scheideggs. Even heavy August storms failed to quench his enthusiasm for the country he regarded as 'the most beautiful, and the one where I want to live if I get to be really old'. So bad were conditions that on one occasion he had to take refuge in a private house, writing that it boasted 'vermin ... a rasping clock which struck the hours with enormous to-do and a baby that bawled the whole night long'. About certain of his travelling companions, he was less sanguine:

Two Englishmen are now sitting next to me and an Englishwoman is sitting on top of the stove. They're as thick as two planks. I've had a journey with them for a few days. All they do is moan that there are no fireplaces. Their whole existence consists of picking on the guide, who laughs at them, quarrelling with the innkeeper and yawning at one another.

At Engelberg, Felix played organ at a service in the Benedictine Abbey, taking his place amid the monks 'a very Soul among the prophets':

An impatient Benedictine at my side played doublebass and others the fiddle, one of the dignitaries being first violin. The *Pater Praeceptor* stood in front of me, sang a solo, and conducted with a long stick as thick as your arm. A decayed old rustic played a decayed old oboe, and at a little distance two more were puffing away composedly at two huge trumpets with green tassels.

Felix made his way back toward Munich following a route that took him over the Simplon Pass, through the Rhône valley, Chamonix and past Lake Geneva, to Interlaken and Vierwalsstattersee. Stopping over at Lucerne, he rested for a while, addressing a mass of letters to family and friends and, in a note to Goethe, giving an amusing account of a poor performance of Schiller's *William Tell*.

He arrived in Munich in September, staying two months, renewing his friendship with Delphine von Schauroth, and giving the première of the piano concerto he had dedicated to her. The same programme, at Odem Hall, included also the first Symphony and the *A Midsummer Night's Dream* overture. At the end, Felix found himself called on to improvise on Mozart's *Non più andrai*. Best of all, he left Munich with a contract in his pocket for an opera commissioned by the city theatre.

Right:
Engelberg.
Left:
Unterseen.
Drawings by
Mendelssohn during his
travels in Switzerland.

Victor Marie Hugo (1802-85). Poet, dramatist and novelist. Leader of romantic movement in France in early nineteenth century.

Niccolo Paganini (1782-1840). Violin virtuoso, who revolutionised the technique of violin playing.

At Heidelberg, he received the happy news that 'fat Rebecka' (as Heine called her) had become engaged. He then went to Düsseldorf to consult with the dramatist Karl Immermann about a suitable libretto for his opera. Both agreed that Shakespeare's *The Tempest* would make an excellent choice, but Felix seems not to have been attracted by Immermann's ideas and the plan was quietly shelved.

The coming winter Felix elected to spend in Paris. The French capital had weathered the revolution of the previous July with considerable finesse. In his attempts to censor the press and corrupt still further an already dubious political system, Charles X had ended up losing his throne.

In August, Louis Philippe was crowned, the ensuing climate — one in which censorship was abolished, the monarchy affirmed as non-legislative, the right to pass laws and adjudged sole right of the chambers, and the role of Catholicism as the state religion brought to an end — producing a flowering in the intellectual and artistic community.

Later the same year, Victor Hugo published his firebrand *Hernani*. A year later, and Stendhal's *Le Rouge et le Noir* and Balzac's *Un Peu Chagrin* came off the presses, while 1832 saw the production of Hugo's satirical *Le Roi s'amuse*. In the visual arts, Daumier, Delacroix and Delaroche were not backward in giving their drawings and painting a political tinge. Life in Paris, Felix wrote home, was a case of politics, politics, and more politics.

At even Gymnase Dramatique, his favourite theatre, sex and politics jostled wit and talent nightly for first place. Young romantics were giving Parisian musical life a definitive stamp. Barely out of their teens, Chopin and Liszt were hammering at the gates. Felix again heard Liszt play and quickly revised first impressions gleaned a few years before. Gregovorious dubbed this titanic youngster 'the centaur pianist', so inseparable did he seem from his piano.

At forty-four, Paganini was a living legend, performing at the *Opera* violinistic feats of such dexterity that with a sinister, cadaverous appearance (the effect highlighted by dark glasses) he seemed an emissary from the devil himself. Among pianists, Thalberg and Kalkbrenner were at their height.

Although he never felt really at home in Paris, Felix this time found the atmosphere of the city more congenial. As usual, he plunged into a whirl of social engagements. He renewed contact with Cherubini and made many new friends, including Habeneck, Ole Bull and Meyerbeer. His closest friend was Hiller. They had many arguments together, usually on the question of French and Italian music, of which Felix was no great lover (he could, in fairness, criticize his compatriots just as well, remarking that Handel had different drawers for his choruses; one labelled 'warlike', another 'heathen', a third 'religious'.)

He also found time to poke his customary fun at the French mania for titles and decorations. To Rebecka, he wrote that everyone seemed to be wearing the *Légion d'honneur* or some such fanci-

Ferdinand Hiller
(1811-85). Pianist and
conductor.

Right:
Frédéric Francois Chopin
(1810-49). Exact
contemporary with
Mendelssohn, the poet of
the piano.

Bottom: Giacomo
Meyerbeer (1791-1864).
Composer of operas
including *Robert Le
Diable*.

ful ribbon, and that only the man who really *had* achieved something was forbidden from wearing it.

Under Habeneck's direction, the Conservatoire Orchestra played
the *A Midsummer Night's Dream* overture. A few weeks later, Felix
appeared to widespread acclaim as soloist in Beethoven's G major
Piano Concerto. Among musicians, he was especially admired for
his Octet and the string Quartets.

It consequently came as a heavy and unexpected blow when the
Reformation Symphony was rejected by the Conservatoire players
as dry and scholastic. Such a shock, in fact, that Felix failed even to
mention the rebuff in his letters home, expressing instead a certain
grim amusement at the way in which, at a memorial service for
Beethoven, the *scherzo* from his own Octet had been played, the
officiating priests functioning solemnly at the altar as the music
tripped gaily on its way.

Despite this disappointment, Felix's second visit to the French capital proved a more fruitful affair than the first. Though never the closest of friends, he cemented with Chopin an admiration that was to prove mutual and lasting. Though he disliked Liszt's music, he showed the younger man his own G minor Piano Concerto, Liszt played it at sight from the manuscript; a feat that caused the usually reticent Felix to exclaim that 'it was a miracle, an absolute miracle ... it could not have been played more beautifully'; Heine he seems to have met and disliked. About Meyerbeer, he was ambivalent. The two may have been on cordial terms in public, but when Felix was told he resembled the older man he had his hair cut and combed a different way.

The winter of 1832 brought personal losses. On 23 January his old violin teacher and friend, Eduard Rietz died. In his memory, Felix wrote the *adagio* that eventually became the second movement of the String Quintet in A. On 22 March came an ever greater loss, the death at eight-two of Goethe. Mendelssohn must have expected the old poet's death, but the news still affected him deeply. He wrote home:

Goethe's loss impoverishes us all. How different Germany now looks! Not all the friendliness here, not all the coming and going, not all the merry life, can cancel the impression left by this news.

It was, on the whole, as a social personality, a performer and an organizer rather than as a composer that Felix made his mark in Paris. The rejection of the *Reformation* Symphony rankled especially. With his reverence for Bach, Felix set special store by his more contrapuntal works, music for which the French, players and listeners alike, seemed to have no use.

A mild attack of cholera added to his problems, but by April Felix was in London again. As soon as he arrived, he realised how much he preferred England's 'sandy rest' to Paris, writing home:

How glad I am to be here, how dear everything seems, how I rejoice in the friendship of old acquaintances.

Once more, he stayed in rooms at 103 Great Portland Street. When he turned up, Klingemann, Moscheles, Attwood and others were there to greet him. Wandering into a Royal Philharmonic rehearsal, someone shouted 'Look, there's Mendelssohn!'. Once more, he went to work with a will, completing his B minor *Capriccio* for piano and orchestra, conducting a further revision of the *Hebrides* Overture and giving two performances of the Piano Concerto.

With Moscheles, he played Mozart's Two-piano Concerto, writing special cadenzas for the occasion. On Sundays, he played the organ at St. Paul's, drawing capacity crowds. It was at this time that Novello published, under the title *Original Melodies for the Pianoforte*, the first collection of *Songs without Words*.

Praise was heaped from all sides, but this was overcast by sadness with the death, in Berlin on 15 May, of Zelter.

With Zelter's death, the directorship of the *Singakademie* fell vacant. The question soon arose as to whether Felix ought to return home and apply for the post. Surprisingly perhaps, he was not burning with desire to clutch the prospect hanging before him. To Rebecka he wrote that if nomination fell into his lap, he would accept it, but that he would not 'lift a finger' to reach for it. Unless his father declared otherwise, he would return home only when his concerts were finished.

Thus it was only around Midsummer, 1832 that Felix made his way back to Berlin and the house at 3 Leipzigerstrasse. On the surface, he seemed more determined than ever to lead the creative life of a composer. The still unwritten opera seems in particular to have nagged at his mind (in recent months he had started to contemplate the life and death of the apostle Paul).

He knew moreover that much as he loved England, Switzerland, and Italy, he could only be a German composer. A few months earlier, he had written his father:

The right moment has arrived to write you a few words about my travelling plans. I do so in a more serious frame of mind than usual. First, let me review what you defined as the purpose of my journey. I was to observe closely various countries and select the one in which I plan to live and work. Further, I was to make my name and capabilities known so that those I finally decided to settle among would receive me and not be wholly ignorant of my capacity. I am happy to say that I believe I have done this. The country is Germany. I am now absolutely certain.

Soon after Zelter's death, however, he wrote more cautiously:

I don't know how I shall get on in Berlin, whether I shall be able to enjoy the same facilities for work, and progress, that are offered to me in other places. The only house that I know in Berlin is our own.

England or Germany? Composition or what? Felix, not for the first time, was unsure of himself and, one senses, divided over what he wanted. The one certainty that seemed to shine out as he hastened home was his vocation as a composer. Little can he have known what lay in store.

Chapter 6

Alarums and Excursions

'It is easier to sail many thousand miles than it is to explore the private sea, the Atlantic and Pacific Ocean of one's being alone: herein are demanded the eye and the nerve' — THOREAU

Conservative, pedantic, unadventurous — Felix's rival as director of the *Singakademie* was Karl Friedrich Rungenhagen, for many years Zelter's assistant and preferred favourite of the *Singakademie* old guard.

Mendelssohn, aged 27.

How much Felix wanted the job is open to doubt. He told Rebecka he would only accept it if it 'fell into my lap'. Yet having returned from London, he found himself willy-nilly pressed on all sides to enter the list of candidates for Zelter's post. The whole family, Abraham, Lea, Fanny, were as one. Even Devrient vigorously concurred. Only Felix was uncertain, writing that Berliners considered him 'an arrogant eccentric'.

The Board of Trustees at the *Singakademie* deliberated from August 1832 until January the following year. This suggests that internal factions were at work, and that a decision proved difficult to reach. Mud was thrown and aspersions cast. As the final meeting drew near, Rungenhagen's supporters mounted a vitriolic campaign against Felix. His age, his inexperience, even his prolonged absence from Berlin, all were cited against him. Some said that Abraham was attempting to 'buy' the *Singakademie*. Others according to Devrient, were overheard to exclaim that 'the *Singakademie* was a Christian institution, and that on this account alone it was unheard of to try and foist a Jew upon them'.

When the voting figures were finally declared, the entire Mendelssohn family were present. A first tally seemed even. But the Rungenhagen vote quickly mounted, and it became obvious that Felix was falling behind. In the end, Rungenhagen picked up 148 votes, Felix a paltry 88. Felix was at the same time offered the vice-directorship, an option he politely declined. Angered by what they saw as a rebuff, the rest of the family the next day resigned en masse from the *Singakademie*.*

The 'respectability' of an academic appointment was however, still the goal, and family pressure for Felix to be up and doing continued.

True, not everything that came his way was unpleasant.

In November 1832, the Royal Philharmonic Society had offered commissions for 'a symphony, an overture and a vocal composition', the performing rights of which would be retained by the society for two years (given the fee, 100 guineas, well might Felix feel that 'the fog is beginning to lift').

The first of these was to be the *Italian* Symphony. The previous fall, Felix expressed acute misgivings over the score but, by April 1833, felt confident enough to deliver it in person, along with two overtures, a revised version of the *Hebrides* Overture and an earlier 'Trumpet' Overture. The vocal piece, the concert aria *Infelice*, would have to wait until 1834.

Nearer home, an invitation came from the Rhineland for Felix to conduct the 1833 Lower Rhenish Music Festival in Düsseldorf the coming May. There was also joyful news from Moscheles. Charlotte, his wife, was expecting a baby and it had been decided that the child should be named after Felix and that he should be godfather.

---

* The choice of Rungenhagen soon proved disastrous. Under his direction, the *Singakademie* went into a sharp decline.

These, then, were some of the reasons for Felix again packing his bags. Stopping off briefly in Düsseldorf, he made his way back to London, conducting on 13 May the première of the *Italian* Symphony with spectacular success. In the same programme, he appeared as soloist in Mozart's D minor Piano Concerto. He also made the acquaintance of little Felix Moscheles. The only disappointment was the cancellation of a series of Beethoven violin sonatas that Felix had been due to play with Paganini. The great violinist had to undergo jaw surgery and withdraw from the project.

No sooner was London dealt with than Felix dashed back to Düsseldorf to prepare for the opening, on 26 May, of the Rhenish Music Festival. A small town on the Rhine, Düsseldorf was packed at Festival time. 1833 was to be no exception, hotels sleeping eight and ten to a room, shops and the inevitable pickpockets alike doing a roaring trade.

Knowing how bitterly Abraham had been disappointed by his son's failure to secure directorship of the *Singakademie,* Felix went out of his way to invite him to attend the Düsseldorf jamboree — a tactful move that led to a renewed intimacy between father and son.

Stimulated by good music and the general bustle, their conversation went on late into the night. Despot he may have been but, at fifty-seven, Abraham was mellowing. This almost certainly had something to do with failing eyesight.

For months past, Abraham had been having trouble with his vision, and by the spring of 1833, was aware that he was going blind. The saving grace was now his pride in Felix, and his letters from Düsseldorf are a vivid testament:

Often I think it miraculous that four hundred people of different nationalities, backgrounds and ages should be blown here all together like driven snow to let themselves be ruled by a youngster without title or official distinction. (The usual noise) happened again during the first rehearsals. Then Felix said that he was not going to stand for it. He was neither able nor willing to shout and it was their duty to listen to him. After he repeated this command I assure you one cannot imagine a more punctilious obedience. The moment he taps his baton and wants to say something, there is a general hush and a deep silence.

The Festival turned out to be a spectacular success, though circumstances were not always as favourable as they might have been. For one, there was the Rhineland summer to contend with. A heatwave, unusually intense even for an area famous for its vineyards, sank down on the city. Irritability and discomfort rose with the thermometer. There was also, on the day of the opening concert, a small but noisy demonstration outside the hall by members of an anti-semitic students' movement, The Blacks *(Die Schwarzen).*

Yet inside, at six o'clock in the evening of 26 May, heat or no heat, the hall was packed for a performance by a crack choir and orchestra numbering over five hundred of Handel's oratorio *Israel in Egypt.* Twelve hundred auditors had come from as far away as

Holland, travelling by stage, Rhine steamer, horseback and on foot. Felix had been rehearsing the piece, day in, day out, with a devotion befitting the young man who had searched London for the manuscript score and found not only the original (in George III's library) but also a valuable textbook on performing practice.

Save breaks for lunch and refreshment, rehearsals as late as two days before the performance, started at eight in the morning and ended at ten in the evening. The dress rehearsal was thrown open to the public. The house was full, and at one point, according to Felix, 'such jubilation broke out as I have seldom witnessed. It took a quarter of an hour before proceedings could continue'. Even then Felix was not satisfied, calling on the day of the concert an extra two-hour rehearsal.

That the performance, along with the rest of the 1833 Festival, was an unprecedented success is testified not only by Abraham's letters, but by press reviews of the day. Most significant among these was the notice furnished by the critic of the *Düsseldorf Zeitung*, none other than the usually sour-faced 'ami de Beethoven', Anton Schindler. Hardly a man to pull punches, Schindler wrote:

I have words only of deep joy and admiration for everything which the artists have accomplished with this music festival. The goodwill and dedication to the noble art of music expressed themselves in the tenacity with which the many strenuous rehearsals were undertaken with a zeal such as I have never before witnessed. The exactness and indefatigable industry of the General Director, the excellent Felix Mendelssohn-Bartholdy, are responsible for the quality of the performance. It is due to him alone that the fifteenth Lower Rhenish Festival was incomparably superior to all preceding ones.

The audience, Abraham reported, consisted of all types. During intervals, everyone rushed into a garden area, where tables and chairs had been set up, to consume 'quantities of bread and butter, May wine,* seltzer-water, curds and whey, etc'.

Even a spate of boring new works could not diminish the general enthusiasm. Anxious that Rhineland should, for the first time, hear Beethoven's *Pastoral* Symphony, Felix found himself hoodwinked into agreeing that the second concert of the Festival should additionally offer an *Easter Cantata* by Ernst Wilhelm Wolff, *Kapellmeister* of Weimar, and a cantata *The Might of Music* by one Peter von Winter. Abraham wrote:

The *Pastoral* went quite well, the Wolff cantata deathly boring. One of the Woringen daughters, a charming girl said that all that need be said about the Wolff and the Winter was that 'the Might could get you angry but the cantata is guaranteed to send you to sleep'.

The girls in the chorus secretly armed themselves with flowers and

---

* *'Maitrank'*, a cup made from Hock and Moselle, flavoured with woodruff and herbs.

at the end of the concert, pelted the young conductor. He was then offered a laurel wreath, refusing, until a large man from the chorus pinned him down and one of 'the Woringen girls' placed it on his head. After much discussion, the committee offered Felix as their own gift a specially designed signet ring, made by the painter, Wilhelm von Schadow.

Such was Felix's success, that the committee further offered him a three-year contract, at 600 gold marks a year, for which he agreed to lead Düsseldorf's church music, to give each season a number of concerts with the resident orchestra and to direct the annual festival.

In the meantime, he again made his way to London, this time with Abraham. On the whole, his father was not able to share his son's enthusiasm for England, admitting that this was largely on account of his poor understanding of the language. 'I'm able only to articulate "How do you do" and "Waiter, a mutton chop",' he wrote, 'and a few other such profundities'. The weather especially got him down:

Today at 9.14 am the sun had just enough power to colour the fog yellow, and the atmosphere looks like smoke during a big fire; 'a very fine morning', my barber said to me. 'Is it?', I replied. 'Yes, a very fine morning'. By midday the fog was victorious and at four o'clock I had to move my table right to the window in order to see not what I was writing, but whether I was writing. Felix is playing the organ at St. Paul's but I can not bring myself to leave my room ... I can only say, London is the richest town and Paris the greatest town I ever saw.

Abraham did, however, leave his room when a chance arose to meet, at the Horsleys, 'la Malibran' and, failing eyesight or no, he seems to have fallen under the willowy twenty-six year old's spell to an almost embarrassing degree. By a strange coincidence, soon after Abraham arrived in London he suffered a leg injury similar to that sustained by Felix on an earlier occasion. Son now nursed father, and the entire summer was spent in the English capital.

Abraham puzzled his family by announcing that he was bringing home with him a promising and handsome young painter, called Alphonse Lovie. This turned out to be Felix, whose unexpected arrival was received with the greatest delight.

One further aspect of the journey is worth recording. At the time, the House of Commons was debating a measure to remove the few lingering legal restrictions against British Jews.

Felix attended the debate, and wrote home that 'this morning the Jews were emancipated. This makes me proud. 187 ayes and 52 noes. This is noble and beautiful and fills me with gratitude to the heavens'.

The two years or so that Felix worked in Düsseldorf were his apprenticeship as a conductor and an administrator. His creative work suffered inevitably, and he snatched enough time to compose only the *Fair Melusina* Overture and the *Rondo Brillante* for piano and orchestra. Opera would have to wait, though he worked fitfully at the oratorio spawned by his interest in the apostle Paul, and spurred by a commission, in 1832, from the *Cäcelian-Verein* in Frankfurt.

As an executant musician, he proved adventurous, widening the city's music repertoire, and raiding libraries and archives for wholly forgotten scores by Lassus, Leo, Palestrina and others, no more than names to most people.

There were, however, setbacks. Before he arrived, Felix thought he would be content to live in a town that seemed to have grown up out of the very heart of a vineyard. In London, he had eulogised Düsseldorf to the Horsley girls:

Mendelssohn showed us, on a panorama of Düsseldorf, which is in a book of the Rhine which the Langs sent us, the place where he is to live, the Belgrave Square of the town he says, and also the fashion-walk where he pretends he shall promenade every day from 1 to 3, dressed in a short coat, and with large moustachios and a small riding whip in his hand. I advised, Mary begged him, not to come over for at least three years to come, at which he looked rather offended and tearful. Mary and Sophy, give him two years, Mama one. He says himself that he shall not think of leaving Düsseldorf (excepting to go to Switzerland with Klingemann) next year, and that Moscheles has offered to conduct his overture at the Phil. He wants to compose a great deal I believe, and I think he had better at the same time compose himself, for his mind wants a little settling in my opinion. He is looking much handsomer than he has yet, for his hair is long again like it was last year, which is so very becoming.

But the Düsseldorfers were inclined to resist much that he had in mind for them. Neither Lassus nor Palestrina seem especially to have appealed. At the opera, he set to work on *Don Giovanni,* insisting on no less than twenty ensemble rehearsals and an increase in ticket prices. As a result, the first night was badly disrupted, the curtain having to be lowered three times in the first act alone in the face of barracking from a hard-up audience. (Felix condemned them shortly as 'mainly beer-house proprietors and waiters; by 4 pm half Düsseldorf is drunk'). Niggled at the results expected of them, a deputation from the orchestra also made it clear they would not again play under Felix.

Once spawned, problems multiplied. Enraged at a slovenly rehearsal of Beethoven's *Egmont,* Felix ripped a full score in two. He suffered twinges of conscience when he discovered that his arrival would mean the displacement of the former director of church music, an old man who had held the post for many years:

A very old and crabbed musician in a threadbare coat was summoned. When he arrived and they started attacking him, he declared that he neither could nor would have better music; if any improvement was required, someone else must be employed; that he knew perfectly well what vast pretensions some people had nowadays. Everything was expected to sound so beautiful [Felix had made it known that he considered 'no epithet suitable for the music which has hitherto been given in Düsseldorf'] — this hadn't been the case in his day, and he played just as well now as formerly. I was really very reluctant to take the affair out of his hands, though there could be no doubting others would do infinitely better. I could not help thinking how I would myself feel were I to be summoned some fifty years hence to some town hall, and spoken to in this way, and a youngster snubbed me, and my coat was seedy, and I had not the remotest idea why the music should be better.

Management problems had a maddening habit of getting in the way of Felix's own music. 'When I sat down to my composing in the morning', he wrote later, 'every hour was punctuated by a ringing of the bell. There were grumbling characters to be soothed, seedy musicians to be engaged — this goes on all day'.

To Devrient, he wrote:

I shall never become an [opera] intendant again, and shall always remember those few weeks. To hell with it! To quarrel with people about two thalers, to be strict with the good ones and indulgent with the bad ones, to make noble faces so that they won't lose the respect they don't even have, to act as if one were angry when one isn't — these are things I cannot and will not do.

His relations with Immermann, director at the Opera, deteriorated sharply. Not only was there the *Don Giovanni* fiasco to contend with. A new theatre was to be opened in Düsseldorf, and Felix had to spend most of August, 1833 auditioning in Berlin the singers Devrient had short-listed for the enterprise.

This resulted in much sordid bargaining and double-dealing of a kind Felix was ill suited to. 'Fräulein Grösser', he fumed, 'will roast in the musical inferno for turning her poetic soul away from us for 500 thaler. How miserable the devils are, we know from *Robert le Diable,* and there it will be still worse'.

The upshot was that, without warning, he threw up his post at the opera house. To Klingemann, he wrote in belligerent mood:

I don't feel the pleasure of reigning. I don't believe in the development of German theatre through Düsseldorf. I don't get along with Immermann. I won't consent to praise mediocrity — and be damned to it.

No doubt Felix had much to put up with, but even so firm a friend as Devrient felt he had failed to handle a difficult situation as well as he might. Accustomed to having his own way, Felix had difficulty brooking disagreement. Abraham took the same view, upbraiding his son with the charge that he had once again 'grabbed things quickly and dropped them quicker':

On your return to Düsseldorf you allowed yourself to be overwhelmed. Instead of striving quietly to remedy your difficulties, you at one leap extricated yourself, and by doing so subjected yourself to the imputation of fickleness and unreliability, and made a decided enemy of a man [Immermann] whom, at all events, policy should have taught you not to displease; and most probably offended and lost the goodwill of many committee members.

All this unpleasantness did not prevent new opportunities arising. An invitation soon arrived asking Felix to supervise a music festival to be held in Cologne in 1835.

In May, 1834 he went to the Lower Rhine Festival at Aachen, where there was a pleasant meeting with Chopin and Hiller. In a

View of Aachen.

letter to his mother, Felix, after praising their playing, adds predictably:

Both, however, rather toil in the Parisian spasmodic and impassioned style, too often losing sight of time and sobriety and of fine music; I, again, do so perhaps too little, but we all mutually learn something and improve each other, while I feel rather like a schoolmaster, and they a little like 'mirliflores' or 'incroyables' [French dandies].

Hiller described how all three went to a party at which Chopin for a long time sat silent and unnoticed. The moment he began to play, everyone else in the room was forgotten.

The late summer of 1834 also brought an offer to become chief conductor of Leipzig's prestigious *Gewandhaus* Orchestra.
Having this time satisfied himself that in accepting the Leipzig appointment a senior man would not be displaced or dispensed with, and that the resident conductor, Christian Pöhlenz, would be compensated, Felix accepted — stipulating carefully, as part of his contract, that he be allowed in each year five or six free months for composition.

Thus to Leipzig Felix went, to the city of Bach, a great university centre, and hub of the German publishing empire; the city of the St. Thomas Church, and its still outstanding choir.

91

In the years preceding Mendelssohn's arrival, Saxony's second city (the capital was Dresden) had been in a period of decline. But thanks to the entry of Saxony, in 1834, into the German Customs Union, Leipzig was beginning to enjoy an upturn in its fortunes. Commerce was its life-blood. The word *Gewandhaus* means literally 'clothing hall'; the orchestra started its life around 1780 playing in the linen merchants' market hall.

When Mendelssohn came to take up his new post in October 1835, Leipzig's narrow, twisting streets and back alleys, lined by houses with high roofs and dominated by a great market square, was overrun with travellers and merchants. Goethe had described Leipzig as 'little Paris', while its most distinguished resident musician, Robert Schumann — angry that Liszt had spoken

Street scene in Leipzig. (Mary Evans Library).

92

contemptuously of the city's lack of princes and countesses — exclaimed, 'Let him take care! We have our own aristocracy — a hundred and fifty bookshops, fifty printing plants, and thirty periodicals'.

Schumann was himself typical of the young, progressive musicians Felix found awaiting him. At twenty-five, Schumann had come from his native Zwickau intending to study law, but turning, with relief, to music. After many problems and delays, he married the pianist Clara Wieck. Still largely unknown as a composer, Schumann was, by 1835, a perceptive critic, publishing a *New Periodical for Music* in which he did battle with all musical mediocrities and philistines.

Felix quickly fell in with Schumann and his circle.*

He discovered early on that the civic authorities meant to keep their promises, giving him a free hand to reorganize Leipzig's musical life, yet allowing him time for composition. Describing his daily routine, he said that he rose early and composed until lunchtime. He would then take a walk, in the afternoon he played the piano, in the evening composed until suppertime.

Unlike the Berliners or the Düsseldorfers, the people of Leipzig in the main, Protestant — seem also to have taken him to heart. In return, Felix laid the foundations of an excellence that were to make the city the musical capital of Europe. At the start, he scored a major success by securing for the *Gewandhaus* players a substantial pay rise. This he achieved despite the fact that standards left, at that stage, something to be desired. Though directed at the Düsseldorf orchestra, Mendelssohn was in no doubt about the poor playing to be heard throughout Germany.

St Thomas Church and School in Leipzig.

---

*As Henry Pleasants remarks (conversation with the author), Mendelssohn and Schumann seem not, however, to have got on together as people. Perhaps Felix was put out by Schumann's heady romanticism. Schumann, for his part, felt Mendelssohn 'lacked sincerity'.

I assure you that on the downbeat they all come in separately, not one decisively, and in the *pianos* it is apparent that the flute plays sharp, and not a single Düsseldorfer can play a triplet clearly, but all play a quaver and two semi-quavers instead, and every allegro leaves off twice as fast as it began, and the oboes play E natural in C minor, and they carry their fiddles under their coats when it rains, and when it's fine they don't cover them at all — and if you once heard me conduct this orchestra, not even four orchestras could drag you here a second time. That is the misery in Germany — the trombones and the drum and the doublebass excellent, everything else quite abominable.

Yet so much did he believe in the raw material now at his disposal, he refused even to join a campaign to raise funds for a monument in honour of Bach until his own musicians were assured better conditions. To Moscheles, he wrote:

I refused to give anything nor would you, had you known all the wheelings and dealings in Germany with regard to monuments. They throw themselves around the names of public figures; they trumpet in the papers. If they wish to honour Handel, Mozart and Beethoven by founding good orchestras and performing their works properly and intelligently, I'm their man. But I don't care for their lumps of stone as long as their orchestras are a stumbling block, nor for their conservatories in which there's nothing worth conserving. My present concern is the improvement of our poor orchestra.

'After no end of letter-writing, soliciting and importuning', he continued, 'I have succeeded in getting their salaries raised'. As a result the *Gewandhaus* orchestra became in a few years one of the finest in Europe.

Even Henry F. Chorley, in whose eyes Felix could do no wrong, was impartial enough to say that his hero did better with the Leipzig orchestra than he did even with the London Philharmonic; an organisaztion that, according to Miles Birkett Foster, Mendelssohn had 'raised, Phoenix-like from the ashes'.

In the Saxon capital, Felix was happy and contented. If the *Gewandhaus* musicians were no virtuosi, he could at least mould them into a flexible and unified body. Rehearsing daily, he instilled a fine *ésprit de corps*. In this, he was helped by Ferdinand David who was called to Leipzig in 1836 as orchestra leader. David later

Illustration in a letter to Ignaz Moscheles, 27.2.1833, in which Mendelssohn promised to give all the orchestral instruments portrayed as his first present to his new godson Felix, son of Ignaz.

provided much advice about the solo part of Mendelssohn's Violin Concerto. Little wonder when, only a few months after taking up his post, Leipzig University conferred on Felix an honorary doctorate in philosophy.

Having assured the well-being of his players, Felix turned his attention to the Bach memorial, electing to give an organ recital at Bach's old church of St. Thomas. After a programme that included the great C minor *Passacaglia,* Schumann reported:

How well Mendelssohn understands the treatment of Bach's royal instrument is well-known, and yesterday he laid before us nothing but precious jewels. A fine summer evening shone through the church windows; even outside, in the open air, many may have reflected on the wonderful sounds, thinking that there is nothing greater in music than the enjoyment of the twofold mastery displayed when one master gives expression to another. Fame and honour to young and old alike!

Mendelssohn also introduced to the *Gewandhaus* the new and un-flamboyant conducting style he had shown in England and per-fected during his short stay at Düsseldorf.

His very first concert, on 4 October, 1835, caused something of a stir. Previously, the orchestra leader had played standing up, relaying to the orchestra signals received from the conductor, who sat at a piano. But now the leader sat throughout, and Mendelssohn assumed the central role standing in front of the orchestra, a slim whalebone baton covered in white leather firmly in his right hand.

For its time, the concert was unremarkable. The *Calm Sea and Prosperous Voyage* Overture preceded a scene and aria from Weber's *Der Freischütz*, Spohr's Eighth Violin Concerto, the Overture and Introduction to Cherubini's *Ali Baba*, and Beethoven's Fourth Symphony. Schumann reported the evening in duly adulatory terms, though expressed reservations about the baton:

(Mendelssohn) stepped out. A thousand eyes flew toward him. The baton disturbs me. In the symphony the orchestra should be like a republic, but it was pleasant to see how (he) anticipated with his eye every shading and how he, the blessed one, swam in front of the common herd.

So popular did the *Gewandhaus* concerts become, that audiences started to complain that the hall was too small. It had fine acoustics, but the seating arrangements were odd. Audiences were placed at right angles to the stage, and split into two sections facing each other. These seats were, moreover, reserved for ladies, compelled to crane their necks if they wanted to see what was happening on stage. The men promenaded and lounged against the walls.

The English soprano Mary Novello (condemned, by Eric Werner, as 'a silly, often unbearable snob') compared the seating arrangements to those found on a London omnibus, and wrote that the women spent their time appraising each other's dresses, while the men appraised the women. Over the entrance, there came to be engraved (with true Teutonic gravity) the inscription *Res severa verum gaudium* — seriousness alone is true amusement.

Looking back at the old concert programmes, one sees that Felix presented Leipzigers with an enormous range and variety of music. There were, for example, all-Beethoven concerts, one including all four *Fidelio* overtures. There was a performance of Beethoven's little-known cantata *Der Glorreiche Augenblick*. There were Mozart symphonies; a Bach-Handel evening; a series of 'Historical Concerts' that featured a cross-section of music from Bach to Viotti and took in the *St. Matthew Passion, Messiah* and *Solomon.* Among contempories featured were Hiller, Lechner, Marschner, Méhul and Sterndale Bennett, Naumann, Righini and Vogler.

Felix was at pains to ensure that his own music never be pushed to the front. It ranked tenth on the scale. He preferred to bring to the fore Schumann's erratic genius, performing two of his symphonies and, no doubt, puzzling over the younger man's unhappy orchestration.

By far his greatest achievement was to première Schubert's last and longest symphony, the 'Great' C major, composed amid the illness and poverty of the composer's last months, and discovered in Vienna by Schumann, amid a pile of mouldering manuscripts kept by Schubert's brother, Ferdinand. It was most carefully rehearsed (during Schubert's lifetime, a run-through by the Vienna Philhar-

Diploma given to Mendelssohn by University of Leipzig, 20.3.1836.

96

monic had ended in a shambles, the insistent string quavers in the finale reducing the players to laughter), and the performance given on 21 March 1839. Felix wrote to Schubert's brother, reporting: 'There was great and sustained applause after each movement. All the musicians in the orchestra were moved and delighted':*

Von Bülow wrote:

I recall the impression — never again so powerful in subsequent performances — which was made on me by the symphony under Mendelssohn's direction. At that time it was not fashionable to place Schubert on the heights of Mount Olympus. He was admired, loved and enjoyed as a minor master, but there were complaints about the expansiveness of his forms and the monotony of the rhythms. But under Mendelssohn's baton, one was not aware of such faults. Simply through his elastic sensitivity and the magnetic eloquence of his gestures, this brilliant leader was able completely to conceal the above-mentioned deficiencies. What wonderful nuances of colour, what intelligent tempi he used! How easily he caused us to glide over the steps of the 'endless' *allegretto*, so that, at the end, the hearer had no conception of the duration of the acoustical phenomenon! For we had just dwelt in eternity in a timeless world.

It is worth recording also that during the Leipzig years, Mendelssohn presented Beethoven's *Choral* Symphony, a score greeted by Smart's London audience at its première with a mixture of enthusiasm and puzzlement, and one which Habeneck and the Paris Conservatoire had rehearsed over a period of three seasons before daring to play in public.

Felix took an intense interest in the city's whole musical life. As we shall see, he was active in the development of Leipzig Conservatory, where he was to be one of the first teachers. He welcomed to Leipzig, Liszt, Chopin and Berlioz. At the time, Chopin had just completed some new *Études*. He and Mendelssohn met to play samples of each other's work with, it seems, less than complete understanding. 'It was', Felix ruefully recalled, 'as if a Cherokee and a Kaffir had met for a chat'. He was happy nonetheless to arrange a programme of Chopin's music at the *Gewandhaus*. There was also a welcome visit from Moscheles.

Amid much trumpeting and ballyhoo Liszt arrived causing, as Felix wrote his mother, 'a mountain of scandal':

Fundamentally I consider him a good, warm human being and a superb artist. Unfortunately his behaviour toward our public upset everyone. The Philistines were worried about the expensive tickets and wanted to make sure that an excellent artist was not going to have too easy a time of it. And those newspaper scribblers! Charges and counter charges, reviews, accusations — this and that all poured down.

I thought the inimical atmosphere could be best cleared if the people here really got to know and hear him. So I decided to give a *soirée* at the *Gewandhaus*. Everybody had such a good time, we all played and sang with such enthusiasm, that the people swore they had never experienced so diverting an evening.

*Peggy Woodford (*Schubert, his life and times*, Speldhurst, 1978) asserts, with other biographers, that the version of the 'Great' C major presented at Leipzig was cut. There is no evidence for this.

Further incidents occurred on Liszt's first visit to Felix's home. Max Müller, pupil of Mendelssohn, and famous later as an orientalist and philologist recalled:

Liszt who was dressed in Hungarian national costume, looked wild and handsome and announced that he had prepared something special for Mendelssohn. He sat down at the piano and played first a Hungarian folk song and then three or four variations on it, each more incredible than the last, all the while swinging to and fro on the piano bench. We stood around, totally overcome. After praising the hero of the hour, one of Mendelssohn's friends said to him, 'Well, Felix now we can pack up! Nobody can play like that. All of us had better give up'! Mendelssohn smiled and when Liszt approached him, saying that now it was his turn, burst out laughing and declared that he was not going to play. Liszt would not take no for an answer, and after some back and forth Mendelssohn said, 'Well, I will play but you mustn't get angry with me'. So saying he sat down and played — what? First the Hungarian folksong then all the variations, reproducing them so accurately that only Liszt himself might have discerned a difference. We were all afraid lest Liszt might feel a little peeved, because Mendelssohn like a real joker, could not prevent himself from imitating Liszt's grandiose movements and extravagant gestures. But Liszt laughed, applauded enthusiastically, and admitted that nobody, not even himself, could have managed such a piece of bravura.

No less spectacular a visit was made by Berlioz. According to Berlioz, he walked without warning into the *Gewandhaus* one afternoon as Felix was rehearsing *The First Walpurgis Night*. Out of touch for twelve years, the two fell into each other's arms.

As we have seen, Felix gave Berlioz every help in staging two concerts at the *Gewandhaus* devoted to his music, engaging extra players to swell the orchestra to suitably Berliozian proportions. Berlioz was amazed and delighted by the skill of Leipzig musicians, but disconcerted to find so much of Mendelssohn's time absorbed in coaching the choir. 'It grieved me', he wrote perceptively, 'to see a great master and virtuoso like Mendelssohn working painstakingly with the choristers engaged in such menial tasks, although it must be admitted that he fulfilled it with unwearying patience, all his remarks being made with perfect sweetness and courtesy'.

At the end of his visit, the two composers solemnly exchanged batons. Felix must have been amused, giving up his usual elegant whalebone stick for what Berlioz gleefully described as his 'heavy oak staff'. Berlioz had been immersing himself in James Fennimore Cooper's *Leatherstocking Tales*, and enclosed with his baton the disconcerting note:

To the Chief Mendelssohn!

Great chief! We have promised to exchange tomahawks. Mine is a rough one — yours is plain. Only squaws and palefaces are fond of ornate weapons. Be my brother! and when the great spirit shall have sent us to hunt in the land of the souls, may our warriors hang up our tomahawks together at the door of the council chamber.

Between 1835 and 1841, Felix spent most of his time in Leipzig, up to his eyes in a multiplicity of activities, large and small. In May 1836,

Chorus from the Opera
Ruy Blas, 1839.

St. Paul was at last premièred at the Düsseldorf Festival. It was a success, though perhaps less sensational than Felix had hoped. An awkward moment near the beginning, when one of the false witnesses missed his lead, was saved by Fanny who was singing among the contraltos and surreptitiously gave him his cue.

1838 was a better year for composition. The Cello Sonata in B flat, the String Quartets in E flat and D from Opus 44, and *Psalm XCV*, all were completed. 1839 was less eventful. The principal compositions were the music for Victor Hugo's *Ruy Blas*, a play that Felix detested, the D minor Piano Trio, the setting of *Psalm CXIV* and some organ fugues, one of which became a movement of his Second Organ Sonata.*

* During the winter of 1838/9, Hiller witnessed 'a curious example of Mendelssohn's almost morbid conscientiousness with regard to the possible perfection of his compositions'. Calling one evening, he found Felix in a state of acute agitation. For hours, it appeared, he had been struggling with a few bars of part-song that would not come right. Scattered over his desk were twenty attempts that would have satisfied anyone else.

1839 also found Felix once more conducting the Lower Rhine Festival at Düsseldorf. Shortly after, there was a visit to Frankfurt, where Felix's unaccompanied part-songs were sung out of doors, with great success. June 1840 saw a festival in honour of the German printer Gutenberg and for this Felix composed the *Festival Hymn* that contains the tune afterwards adapted in England (by Dr. W.H. Cummings) as the carol, *Hark! The Herald Angels Sing.* Also completed was the 'symphony-cantata' (as Klingemann called it), *Hymn of Praise.*

The greatest sorrow of the Leipzig years came suddenly and without warning on 19 November, 1835. A few weeks earlier, a family reunion at 3 Leipzigerstrasse had seen much pleasant gaiety. Abraham was by now quite blind, but his health otherwise had given no cause for anxiety.

It came therefore as a shock to Felix when, shortly after his return to Leipzig, Hensel hurried over to tell him of his father's death.

Felix at once went to his mother in Berlin. His father had been taken ill the night before his death, but the doctors had sensed no immediate danger. His passing, for all its suddenness, was peaceful and painless.

Unweeping, distracted to a point where Fanny feared for his sanity, Felix returned after ten days to Leipzig, shut himself up, and emerged only to work with the orchestra. To Klingemann, he wrote:

'What all of us have lost, and particularly I, you must realize because you knew him. He loved you. In what manner my life can go on I've no idea, not as yet'.

Fanny added a postscript. 'You know how he worshipped father'. To Pastor Bauer, he wrote that his father had in recent years been his one true friend.

For the rest, Felix's years at Leipzig were largely a success story. At the end of the 1839/40 season, Schumann wrote:

One must confess that in this Leipzig — which nature has treated so shabbily — German music blooms to such a degree that, without arrogance, it can compare with the richest and largest orchards and flower gardens of other cities. What a great abundance of great works of art were produced for us last winter!

How strange, how ironic, that within the year, the cause of this flowering was to accept an engagement that would tear him away from Leipzig; one that would, in the end, bring him only frustration and to near disaster.

But in 1837, a ray of light had poured into Felix's life, with his marriage — an event as sudden as it was unexpected.

Chapter 7

Cécile

'I feel as though I ought to lay my hands on your head and pray to God to keep you so; pure and beautiful and gracious' — HEINE

Four years his senior, the woman Felix loved the deepest, who understood him best, whose feelings were nearest his own and who was from childhood his inseparable friend and confidante, was his sister Fanny.

Intimate, cajoling, and revealing always the tenderest concern, Fanny's thoughts and letters followed him round Europe. Fanny was, for Felix, all at once the luminous Madonna, the 'mother confessor', the eternal woman, the sounding board and the yardstick against which he could measure his ideas, his hopes and his fears.

Fanny Hensel. Drawing by Wilhelm Hensel.

Not for a moment, in the midst of fame or after he had found a wife, did Felix's love for Fanny waver. The evidence for this love is everywhere to be found. Its strength — its passion, even — is unmistakable, on occasion highly-charged. Their correspondence sometimes reads like a series of love letters. When he was fifteen, Felix wrote, 'My sweet — I love you terribly'. From Munich six years later, he sent her a song specially composed, revealing in a covering letter that thinking of her made him feel 'quite giddy'. Only three days before, he had written to his 'darling little sister'.

As for Fanny, her feelings came especially close to the surface when her brother first left home for anything more than a summer vacation, and set out for London. A diary entry reads, 'I stayed with Felix, helping him get dressed and packed. It was very cold. I followed him with my glance until he disappeared from view'.

In March the following year, she wrote to a friend in England that she did not know what she would do without him. 'All will be mute and desolate'.

In Fanny's diary, there are more entries about Felix than Wilhelm Hensel, the man she was to marry. In one letter, she wrote that 'a bridegroom is no more than a man'; while Rebecka could write Felix that 'last night — in lovely moonlight — during charm-

Gioacchino Antonio Rossini (1792-1868). Composer of operas including *The Barber of Seville* and *William Tell*.

ing conversation, by the side of the most ardent betrothed, Fanny fell fast asleep ... Why? Because you're not here!'.

The letter Felix found awaiting for him at Hamburg on the day of his departure for England is illuminating:

Although we wrote as late as yesterday, I still have the desire to send a few lines on this, the last day before you board. You will at this time have to think of me and my state of mind. All that goes without saying. It's the old story.

Even on her wedding day, later the same year, Fanny wrote:

I have your portrait before me, and ever repeating your dear name, and thinking of you as if you stood at my side, I weep! Every morning and every moment of my life I'll love you from the bottom of my heart, and I'm sure that in doing so I shan't wrong Hensel.

Submitting each new composition to his sister for approval, Felix called her his Talleyrand, an 'angel', his fount of inspiration. At the same time, they shared a common sense of humour. Once, in Vienna, Felix sent his sister as a birthday greeting what purported

102

to be a letter from her 'devoted admirer', Beethoven. 'At my age and in the isolation of my empty chambers, I get ideas in my head such as would not be to everyone's taste. I send you as a token my Sonata in B flat major, Op 106 [the *Hammerklavier*]. Some time when you have real leisure, play the sonata. I enclose an awful picture of myself. I consider myself not such a bad fellow'.

By the end of 1835 though, Felix must have felt the time for jesting was over. He was twenty-six. His father was dead. Friends would call on him and try to cheer him up, yet neither friends nor activity could dispel the depression that descended on him.

Returning to his rooms of an evening he would, he complained, feel lonely and out of sorts. Save for a few notes for *St. Paul,* 1835 had seen the composition of no new works.

If he did not even now set out actively to look for a wife, he was certainly more receptive than at any time in the past. Life, it seemed, was more than gentle flirtation and glances exchanged with doe-eyes across the supper table. If he did not soon find a partner, it would mean a life of crusty, dissatisfied bachelordom, a life ending perhaps, like Beethoven's, in illness, loneliness and higgledy-piggledy squalor.

Like summer lightning, love for Felix came unexpectedly. In the fall of 1836 he travelled to Frankfurt to conduct the Cäcilian-Verein in place of Schelble, who was ill. (Hiller was living locally, and coincidentally the melancholic but witty Rossini turned up and charmed Felix as much as he had earlier repelled him. The younger composer seems to have been displeased only when Rossini, with some justice, pointed to the influence of Domenico Scarlatti on Mendelssohn's F sharp minor *Capriccio*. Hiller thought the comparison valid. Felix did not).

Postscript of a concert at Frankfurt. Sketch by Mendelssohn.

The first indication that something was afoot comes in a letter to his sister Rebecka:

The present period is a very strange one, for I am more desperately in love than I ever was in my life before, and I do not know what to do. I leave Frankfurt the day after tomorrow, but I feel as if it would cost me my life. At any rate I intend to return here and see this charming girl once more before I return to Leipzig. But I haven't an idea whether she likes me or not, and I do not know what to do to make her like me, as I have already said. But one thing is certain, that to her I owe the first real happiness I have enjoyed this year. Now you see, I have let you into a secret, which nobody else knows anything about.

It was Hiller and a Dr. Speiss, a Frankfurt surgeon, who were on the receiving end of most of Felix's feelings. 'Lying on the sofa in my room after dinner', Hiller wrote, 'or taking long walks in the mild summer nights with Dr. S and myself, he would rave about her charm, her grace, and her beauty!'

Just nineteen, Cécile Jeanrenaud was of Huguenot descent, the daughter of a pastor in the French reform church. She was fair and blue-eyed, with a tanned skin and an eye-catching figure, 'rather drooping, like a flower heavy with dew', and it is amusing to find Felix at one point writing to her mother that he actually avoided walking with Cécile in the streets of Berlin because of 'the continuous staring of passers-by ... not a man we encounter doesn't open his eyes wide. Cécile often laughs about it and says it isn't meant for her . . .'. A no less glowing testimonial comes from Heinrich Brockhaus:

At the concert I was quite transported by the performance of the concerto by Mendelssohn. His bride was there — that explains his being inspired. The girl, who sat quite close to me, could really inspire one: a charming apparition ... beautiful ... I could gaze at her for ever.

Friendly and vivacious, but of a placid and gentle disposition, Cécile endeared herself to Felix initially by remarking that prior to their meeting, she had imagined him to be an irascible old man, sitting at the organ with a velvet cap on his head, churning out interminable fugues.

At first, Felix seems to have been in two minds. He was strongly attracted to Cécile, but courted her only with diffidence. Only after a vacation at Scheveningen on the Dutch coast with his painter friend, Schadow — during which he spent much of his time lying on the beach thinking over the future — did Felix decide finally that the relationship showed enough promise for him to propose marriage.

The engagement was announced in September 1836, and the ceremony took place at Frankfurt's Walloon French Reform church in March the following year to the accompaniment of a wedding chorus for women's voices specially composed by Hiller.

In the meantime, Felix had at Christmas endeared himself to Cécile by giving her a handsome souvenir album, in which she continued a previously started collection of Goethe manuscripts and autographs.

For their honeymoon, they elected not to travel far afield, visiting Freiburg and keeping together a diary. For the most part, this records people met and places visited, but here and there crops up an entry to remind us that Felix and his bride were two young, painfully inexperienced people, coming to terms with each other for the first time:

Felix and Cécile together in a carriage. Drawing by Mendelssohn from honeymoon diary. (Bodleian).

On our way (to the fortifications) we saw a very pretty flower girl, and Felix noticed at once and turned round several times to look at her. That and a few indifferent words and gestures were sufficient to render me melancholy and jealous ... we began to climb the mountain behind the inn. Felix complains of pains, I behaved very badly ... my mood becomes ever blacker and angrier ... I weep copiously, torturing him and myself ... now we come once again as before. I tell all my silly fears and he is again sweet and gentle with me ... during the whole evening Felix plays all my favourite compositions to me. [at the foot of this entry, Felix adding a touching gloss: Don't be angry with me, dear Cécile].

To the Frankfurt forest ... Felix enjoys all that going to and fro and riding under the trees ... then (he) sits down in his room and scribbles one little musical dot after the other till the end of the day.

He is working steadily as always. What I'm doing is so unimportant that I can't remember ... On Monday, I feel quite unwell, lie around on the bed and on the couch ... Felix takes care of me and spoils me, as does my mother.

The weather this evening is magnificent and the whole landscape lies before us without a trace of fog. We lay under the young trees which are planted around the church, sing, dance on the thin grass, count the islands in the Rhine ... and love each other very much.*

Cécile Mendelssohn née Jeanrenaud.

* The diary is now in the Bodleian Library, and with it a little nosegay of violets which Cécile picked near Ebenach. 'It was I who saw them first, and I picked all I could reach through the bars of a gate. They were for his buttonhole'.

106

A late breakfast. Drawing from Mendelssohn's honeymoon diary. (Bodleian).

During their honeymoon, Felix completed his setting of *Psalm XLII* and his String Quartet in E minor; also, a pleasant little piano *Allegretto* for Cécile that was never published.

A curious aspect of their early life together is that Felix seems to have side-stepped a meeting between **Cécile** and his family. They did not come to the wedding, nor did Felix include Berlin on the honeymoon itinerary. It was Fanny who eventually complained to Cécile that 'for eight months now he (Felix) has a wife I don't know'. Finally she visited Leipzig to meet Cécile for herself, all hint of jealousy put aside when she found her so even-tempered a wife, 'a fresh breeze, so bright and natural', and, she concluded, an excellent foil for Felix's restless nature.

That Felix did not slow down is, however, shown by the fact that months after their honeymoon he had again dashed across the Channel, and spent two weeks in such a flurry of activity, revolving in the main around the Birmingham Festival, that the fortnight might be thought the last of his life. Complaining to Hiller that he wished he were 'sitting with Cécile and had let Birmingham be Birmingham, and could enjoy life more than I do today', he played the organ in Christ Church college. He put the finishing touches to rehearsals of *St. Paul* at Exeter Hall. He played with customary brilliance his Piano Concerto, led the Birmingham Festival, was presented with a silver snuff-box by the Sacred Harmonic Society. At the cathedral he once again played the organ, on this occasion not without an amusing incident:

There was a huge mass of people. I could hardly get to the organ, even though the service had ended. After I had played half an hour the audience increased rather than decreased. Suddenly, at the final passage [of Bach's A minor Prelude and Fugue], there was no air in the organ. Cooper ran away like a man possessed, finally coming back with the information that the man who pumps the bellows had simply given up and gone off. Now I had the chance to observe the public spirit of the English. There was a tremendous outcry as if something really important had happened, and from all corners one heard cries of, 'Shame! Shame!'. Three or four clergymen appeared and gave the beadle a grilling in front of everyone.

There then followed a headlong dash home. Leaving Birmingham at midday, directly after a morning concert, he arrived in London toward midnight. Within the hour, he was in the mail-coach for Dover, arriving at nine in the morning. Disdaining breakfast, he immediately set sail for Boulogne. Suffering, as usual, the effects of sea-sickness he elected nonetheless, without rest or sleep, to travel through Belgium to Cologne.

There he took a steamer down the Rhine, intending to rest for the first time in nearly a week. But in the middle of the night he woke to find that the noise of the engines had stopped and that the steamer was fogbound. With no further ado he rose, dressed, collected his belongings and, with the help of two sailors, found a coach, turning up in Koblenz at three in the morning. Frankfurt, where Cécile was awaiting him, he reached some twelve hours later.

Still the journey was not over, with three more days spent *en route* for Leipzig. They arrived just after lunch on the day Felix was scheduled to conduct the opening concert of the season. And conduct he did, mounting the rostrum sharp at six o'clock. His only comment on this superhuman effort was to concede at the end of the concert that he felt just 'a little *kaput*'

Yet out of this fragmented honeymoon there developed a marriage as strong as it was enduring. For the ten years remaining him, Felix gave every impression of happiness and domestic contentment.

Cécile bore him five children, four of whom survived to adulthood. Only a few details of their married life together escaped destruction, (Cécile burnt much), but those that remain provide touching evidence of their love for one another.

With her gentleness and docility, and her worship of a man she knew to be not only a genius but a kind and good husband, Cécile provided Felix with a degree of security any man could envy.

Like Alice Elgar many years later, she seems happily to have accepted that the care of a genius was 'enough of a life's work for any woman'. From the last years we have a few letters. From Felix:

I can only write to you today and would like so much to speak to you, to kiss you, to spend the whole day with you, to gaze at you, to enjoy [your birthday], to celebrate my happiness and to wish you happiness. If I were with you I'd kiss you ever so often. You'd have to notice me because the whole day I wouldn't leave you in peace. I hope to take the first train on Saturday and at half past two to be where I belong, with my darling, wonderful Cécile.

From Cécile:

Time hangs heavily till you announce your return. My treasure, why don't you write a few lines ... is it a revenge for my stupid joke at Naumberg?

A faithful husband, Felix tried to please Cécile in a hundred ways. He even cajoled Chopin, whose music she loved, to write and sign a few bars of music specially for her. Perhaps the most touching witness is to be found in just two letters. The first is from Felix to Cécile's mother:

When I am with her I do not understand how indispensible to my life, every moment of it, she is. But every time I am away from her, the absence becomes heavier to bear, more insupportable. I patiently count the hours till I shall see her again, her without whom I no longer know gladness or happiness.

The second was written by Cécile a few days after Felix died:

There are corners of my mother-in-law's garden where I must martyr myself to be able to grasp what has happened. Here are the same trees, bower, branches, there is the ruined fountain, and they all still exist. Felix's grave bears a marble cross with his name. Behind it I have planted a lilac and a rosebush. I wanted to keep the mound free and green, but it's always heaped with flowers and wreaths. I placed my tributes at his feet.

With Felix's death, Cécile's own life went into eclipse. Within six years, she too, at thirty-six, was no more. If anyone died from a broken heart it was surely Cécile Mendelssohn.

Chapter 8

Son and Stranger

In the ground,
In the wood
Stands a thornbush.
The winds scatter its leaves
One after another,
Shedding its berries
In the snow
— JACOBSEN

A bitter and repressive monarch, Wilhelm III of Prussia died at last
in 1840. At forty-five, his successor, Friedrich Wilhelm IV could
not, Prussians concluded, be worse than his father. With his
interest in social reform and the arts he was welcomed, especially
by the young.

The times looked propitious. Prussia by 1840 was making great
headway industrially. The German Customs Union of 1834 took
on a special significance with the construction of a new and important rail network. Running from Dresden and Leipzig to Magde-
burg, the first main line was to open the year that Wilhelm IV was
crowned.

Banking expanded to keep pace with the industrialisation that
grew up round a flourishing communications system (most German
cities west of the River Oder were linked by railways within a
decade).

At the same time, through the promptings of a gifted political
philosopher, Friedrich List, moves were afoot for the creation of a
pan-Germanic union, to be called *Middle Europe,* a united states of
Germany, bound together by free trade and a comprehensive trans-
port scheme.

In the event, Wilhelm IV, a figure from whom much had been
expected, proved a sad disappointment, losing himself in dreams of
medievalism and chivalry and eventually (like Wagner's patron,
Ludwig II of Bavaria) becoming incurably insane. As Golo Mann
summarises:

110

He was intelligent, full of good intentions, educated, longed for affection and was appreciative of beauty. But he was weak and a prey to temporary influences, a complacent improvisor, dependent on advisors whom he liked to dupe, superstitious, arrogant and faithless. His ideas were those of a romantic at odds with his age. He wanted to rule with the consent of the people, but this consent must find medieval expression and society must be a hierarchy consisting of happy peasants, honest townsmen, pious clergy, faithful nobles, the prince among his nobles. There could be no such society.

In addition, Wilhelm IV was the most heedless of dilettantes, dropping ideas as quickly as he picked them up.

Among these was his decreee, issued shortly after his succession, commanding that a blueprint be drawn up to mastermind Berlin as the capital city of German culture.

Advised by Humboldt and Bunsen, plans for a comprehensive Academy of Arts were put in motion. There were to be four divisions, architecture, music, painting and sculpture and it was for the directorship of the second of these that Bunsen now recommended 'Germany's most famous living composer', Mendelssohn.

Having sounded out the 'sensible' Mendelssohn, Paul, His Excellency Ernst von Massow, the King's deputy, approached Felix with a proposal. Under its terms Felix would be retained as director of the music class of the Academy; composer for the Royal Theatre; director of the Royal Orchestra; and conductor and organiser of the Cathedral choir. He was, in short, being invited to plan and control the whole range of Berlin's musical life.

Berlin. Unter Den Linden. Detail of painting by Wilhelm Brücke, 1842.

111

The idea was a heady one but, flattered though he was, Felix at first was diffident. Bureaucracy in general, Berlin bureaucracy in particular, he knew only too well:

The Berlin proposal is very much on my mind and I think about it quite a bit. I'm still doubtful that it will lead to a result which both of us envisage. I still doubt that Berlin is the place where an artist like myself can feel at home, despite all the honours and money. Yet the very fact that it has been offered gives me a push and a certain satisfaction. I feel that I have been awarded an honour.

Only a few weeks later, he wrote Klingemann an unusually long letter in which he again expressed misgivings about giving up Leipzig for the Prussian capital, and frankly begged his friend to advise him, 'I'm interested in composing a variety of new works', he wrote, and believe me, I know that an official post could hinder me in my main endeavour, if not destroy it. Advise me soon ... what do you say? Does the call of Berlin appeal to you or not?'

Quite apart from this uncertainty, Mendelssohn felt also that the standard of musical performance in Berlin was far lower than that which he had established in Leipzig. Devrient's account makes it clear that this was the case. The prevailing influence at the opera, for example, was that of Spontini. Altogether, it was a period of false splendour, ruinous to the spirit of German music. Spontini had little idea. The violent contrasts in which he sought his effects, the startling shocks of his *sforzati* — in fact, all his effects — seemed calculated to tell only on the nerves and senses of the listeners, and could not but demoralise his orchestras.

Clearly at a loss to know what advice to give, Klingemann delayed his reply for nearly four months. When it at last arrived, it was couched in very cautious terms. His view was that Felix might just consider acceptance, adding, finally, 'Why cannot you create that magnificent peace and quiet of yours in Berlin? Think about it'.

Felix did and, in possibly the unhappiest single decision of his life, accepted the post. Just why remains unclear, but a few possible explanations can be put forward.

In the first place, had the appointment succeeded it would, despite his protestations to the contrary, have been a crowning achievement both for Felix and German music. The invitation was, after all, a tangible recognition of his genius. With the free hand he had been given in Leipzig, had he not achieved a great deal? With the right kind of safeguards, might it not be possible to do the same in the Prussian capital and, moreover, build a musical community even closer to his heart's desire?

The challenge represented by the Berlin appointment must also have appealed to Mendelssohn's hyper-active nature. At the time, the capital city was not short of distinguished eccentrics who hurled themselves into the business of living like madmen, there was, for example, a Dr. Heim, who had no fewer than 1,400 patients and could be consulted at five in the morning while he shaved. He died, still racing from one appointment to the next, at the ripe age of eighty-seven. Anything they could do, Felix could to better.

As Felix admitted, there was the attraction of living once more close to his family. And, above and beyond all these considerations, he must have had in mind the fact that the offer had come from the King. Well might Felix poke fun at official stupidity, but he was nonetheless, in Montaigne's phrase, dazzled by 'the strange lustre that surrounds a king'. Then there was the question of salary. An increase from 1000 thaler a month in Leipzig to 3000 thaler a month in Berlin must have attracted even a man who had inherited a fortune.

The Minister of Arts, von Eichorn (a figure dismissed by Fanny as being 'as weak as a mouse') acted as an intermediary throughout the negotiations. Through him, Mendelssohn insisted on certain conditions of which the two most important were that he would accept the Berlin appointment for a year only, on a trial basis, and that during that time he would not resign from the *Gewandhaus* at Leipzig. These terms were approved, and as a result Felix and his family in 1841 moved back to Berlin.*

It was about this time that Felix came into contact with another of Germany's rising stars in the musical world, Richard Wagner. The relationship proved profitless, and neither seems especially to have liked the other. As early as 1836, the twenty-three old Wagner had written Felix a courteous letter enclosing the manuscript score of his C major Symphony which, he suggested, Mendelssohn might like to perform.

The *Gewandhaus* orchestra had, however, already played the piece, and Mendelssohn was not inclined to re-stage a work he evidently disliked. After his death the score, unreturned to Wagner, could not be found either among Mendelssohn's papers or at the *Gewandhaus* archives. The Symphony was reconstructed eventually and published from orchestral parts, found in a trunk in Dresden, when Wagner fled the city in 1849. Wagner is supposed subsequently to have railed at the admittedly unreliable Du Moulin Eckhart that Mendelssohn had deliberately destroyed the score because 'he detected in it a talent that was disagreeable to him'.

In *My Life*, Wagner wrote that on the occasion of his eventually working with Mendelssohn for a concert in Leipzig he 'became conscious of the peculiar interest and excitement with which this master of music who, though still young, had already reached the zenith of his fame and life's work, observed or rather watched me'. Mendelssohn, Wagner concluded, was jealous over his own triumph in the opera house with *Rienzi,* and resentful of the fact that Devrient 'whose gifts he acknowledged should now so openly and loudly sound my praises'. In the same vein, Wagner further complained that because he, Wagner, was conducting two arias from

*The omens were, however, already ominous. Shortly before leaving Leipzig, Felix wrote the Scottish composer George Macfarren (whose *Chevy Chase* overture had recently been given at the *Gewandhaus),* 'God bless you, my dear Sir; excuse these hasty lines; they pack up all my things, and I am in a black, at least a greyish, mood'.

Rienzi, Felix deliberately programmed his own *Ruy Blas* Overture because it too was operatic'.

Yet despite his later anti-semitic tirades, Wagner respected Mendelssohn's skill. There are letters in which the young composer-to-be of the *Nibelung* saga, wrote 'My dear, dear Mendelssohn, I'm really happy you like me'. After the Berlin première in 1844 of *The Flying Dutchman* he wrote his then wife, Minna:

Mendelssohn, with whom I dined once, gave me great pleasure; after the performance he came onto the stage, embraced me, and congratulated me most heartily.

A year earlier, Wagner had written to Mendelssohn that he was 'proud to belong to the nation which produced you and your *St. Paul*'.

It was only when Wagner grew older and started to dictate his voluminous memoirs to his second wife Cosima, that his malevolence was given full rein, and he began muttering that Leipzig (whose earlier standards he had deplored) would have done well to return to a 'non-Judaic age'.

In 1855, he had made the mistake of conducting Mendelssohn for a London audience. After the concert, Wagner raved at the press, saying that they were a load of Jews, and wrote to Ernst Kietz a vitriolic letter in which he claimed that he was 'being torn apart by the press over Mendelssohn and other Jews who would like to pack me off to eternal life. Conducting the concert (this evening) I kept my gloves on for a very bad symphony of Mendelssohn [the *Italian*]. For (Weber's) *Euryanthe* Overture, I took them off'.

Mendelssohn, for his part, seems to have agreed with Schumann who, on reading through *Tannhaüser,* declared that Wagner was incapable of writing four bars consecutively that were melodious or even correct.

The next year, Felix conducted at the *Gewandhaus* an 'ostentatiously ill-humoured' performance of the overture.

At the time of his return to Berlin, Mendelssohn's relationship with Wagner, however much it may have lacked in warmth, was, however, correct and formal.

He had, besides, other, more pressing problems to deal with, the most important being the lack of progress made with the Academy project. Having initiated the idea, Wilhelm IV appeared quickly to lose interest. Mendelssohn's ideas were never rejected outright. They were simply shuffled from one office to another, coming to rest finally in some obscure and inaccessible locker. A letter to Klingemann reveals his frustration:

Grand plans, tiny achievements, sophisticated critics, miserable musicians; liberal ideas and the streets full of court employees. I doubt that I shall be able to stand it for more than a year.

A glutton for punishment, Felix was in fact, for five years to remain nominally in the King's employ, wrestling continuously with the twin problems of insufficient funds and 'miserable' musicians.

Title page of the score of the incidental music for Sophocles' *Antigone* by Mendelssohn, 1841. (British Museum).

Not surprisingly, his composition during this period lacked the sparkle and originality of his earlier work. Apart from the interesting but uneven music to Racine's *Athalie* and Sophocle's *Antigone*, and the Cello Sonata in D, the most important examples from those depressing years in Berlin were the *Variations sérieuses* for piano and the incidental music for *A Midsummer Night's Dream*, written at the King's behest for a production at Potsdam.

Not the least remarkable part of this latter achievement is the way in which Felix was able to produce twelve new numbers (including a *Nocturne, Intermezzo, Scherzo,* the *Wedding March* and the chorus *Ye Spotted Snakes),* worthy to be placed alongside the overture composed seventeen years before.

Despite a less than wholly successful production in Potsdam — the King indulged in an endless intermission, during which tea was served in the royal box, and then managed to disturb the introduction to the third scene by noisily clattering spoons — the incidental music soon enjoyed a runaway success.

In Berlin, the entire Mendelssohn family attended the opening night, and, so Fanny reported, monopolised two rows of balcony seats. At the end, the audience began calling for Mendelssohn and, rather than let them down, Paul took a bow for his brother. Once again, it was Fanny who pointed out Felix's accomplishment:

We were saying yesterday what an important part the *Midsummer Night's Dream* has always played in our home, and how we had all at different times gone through all the parts from Peaseblossom to Hermia and Helena, and now it's come to such a glorious culmination. We were really brought up on the *Midsummer Night's Dream*, and Felix especially made it his own, almost recreating the characters that had sprung from Shakespeare's creative genius. From the *Wedding March*, so full of pomp but so thoroughly festive in character, to the plaintive music of Thisbe's death, the fairy songs, the dances, the interludes, the characters, including such creatures as clowns — all and everything has found its counterpart in music, and his work is on a par with Shakespeare's.

Not even the popular success of *A Midsummer Night's Dream* could, however, reconcile Felix to Berlin, with its unrewarding grind and catalogue of unfulfilled promises. To add to his gloom, in December 1842 Lea died, only a few hours after she had acted as hostess to a large and convivial gathering. Felix mourned her as deeply as he had the passing of his father. When the news came, he was in Leipzig, and wrote to his brother Paul that he was trying to carry on his regular work, adding that 'half mechanical work' transcribing and copying, was helping him to find relief from depression. He was, he said, grateful for the 'pleasant intercourse with the old familiar oboes and violas and the rest, who live so much longer than we do, and are such familiar friends'.

In May the following year, Felix and Wagner found themselves both contributing pieces for the unveiling at Dresden of a statue of the late King Friedrich August I of Saxony. Wagner's setting was for unaccompanied men's voices, while Mendelssohn's used, with all the hallmarks of hard work, a male voice chorus and brass. We have it on Wagner's authority that his own 'simple and heartfelt composition eclipsed entirely the complex artificialities of Mendelssohn'.

By 1844, Felix was at the end of his tether, and went to the King and announced that he was returning to Leipzig. Professing surprise (according to Adolf Marx, Wilhelm could talk as persuasively as 'a travelling salesman') the King at last consented, asking only that Felix make himself available for special occasions.

Leipzig welcomed Felix back with open arms, and he at last followed through a project he had long had in mind — the foundation of a really first-rate Conservatory of Music. In the spring of 1832, Felix had been appointed *Kapellmeister* to the King of Saxony. From this post he had now resigned but, working with the support and encouragement of the Saxon court, Leipzig's Conservatory came into being and to this day remains among Europe's foremost centres of musical education.

In addition to administering the school, Felix took piano and composition classes. Sir George Grove has given a vivid description of the latter. As a teacher, Felix was keen and stimulating, but fastidious. It is not surprising to read of him speaking, in English, to an English pupil, of a certain 'very ungentlemanlike modulation'. Kupferburg tells of an occasion when Felix wrote on a blackboard a theme around which he then invited a student to invent an appropriate counterpoint. On this occasion, his pupil found it impossible to add even a single note, and said so. 'You can't tell where to put the next note?', Mendelssohn asked, 'well, neither can I!'.

For his Conservatory, he gathered a distinguished faculty. Ferdinand David taught violin, Niels Gade and Schumann composition, Moritz Hauptmann taught harmony and counterpoint, Carl Ferdinand Becker organ, and Christian August Pöhlenz singing. Ignaz and Charlotte Moscheles took charge of the piano department.

Felix insisted that poverty should not debar the talented student. In a memorandum to the Conservatory's sponsors, he wrote that 'the most admirable talent' was to be found among students rarely 'possessing the means to pay for private lessons'. Scholarships, he insisted, were essential, and it is satisfying to note that among the first to seize this opportunity was a twelve-year old violin prodigy from a Viennese family by the name of Joseph Joachim. Mendelssohn recognised in young Joseph an extraordinary talent, going so far as to accompany him in recitals. When he died in 1907, full of years, Joachim was regarded as the foremost violin master of the age.

Another joy during this second Leipzig period, was Felix's completion of the E minor Violin Concerto, ideas for which had plagued him for five and more years, and the beginning of which, he wrote to David, 'gives me no peace'.

Yet, pleased as he was to be back in Leipzig, pleased as he was to be taking up the threads of composition again, pleased as he was to

Left:
Moritz Hauptmann
(1792-1868).

Right:
Ferdinand David
(1810-1873).

be involved in the launching of the new Conservatory, Felix was beginning perceptibly to tire.

When a courtier repeated the old chestnut about *A Midsummer Night's Dream* being an unworthy vehicle for such fine music, Felix could respond only with sarcasm. As for the Berlin *debacle*, Felix could only feel that he had failed, that he had 'let the side down'.

The wasted effort, the frustration of it all, can only be guessed. Felix was first to recognise that his creative flow had been hampered by the years of to-ing and fro-ing round the Prussian court.

It is still said that his invention had in any case begun to run dry, though this is unlikely. It was more a question of fatigue and a growing sense of inadequacy. When he retreated from Berlin a second time, Fanny wrote ingenuously that Felix, 'has once again become loveable'. To Devrient, he could jest that 'the first step out of Berlin is a step toward happiness'.

But twice had he mounted assaults on the capital of Prussian culture, twice had he failed. And that was something Felix Mendelssohn could hardly begin to comprehend.

Chapter 9

Victoria and Albert, Jenny Lind, *Elijah*

'A wonderful genius ... so pleasing and amiable' — QUEEN VICTORIA

Of Mendelssohn, Henry F. Chorley wrote, 'There has never been a foreigner more honest in his love for, more discriminating in his appreciation of England'. 'If you wish to enjoy a great success', Chopin chimed in during a visit to London, 'you have to play Mendelssohn'.

Debonair, graceful, fine-tempered, Felix's music gave the Victorian English what they wanted. In George R. Marek's words it was, in the best sense, *eau de cologne,* 'sweet-smelling but not too heady'.

Only recently has it been possible to see the Victorian age in some kind of perspective. No generality can fairly be applied to so various an era, yet a few characteristics may be picked out.

Its social compass was remarkably wide. At one end of the scale was the immaculately turned out Count D'Orsay (the 'Phoebus Apollo of dandyism' Carlyle called him), gambling away his fortune at Crockford's, and making ardent love to Lady Blessington! At the other, was the great mass of the poor. Within this compass, there grew up a middle-class and an urban working class divided in politics but, by and large, devoted to Queen, country and *Pax Britannica.*

About 1840, a Lancashire cotton-printer called Thomson, accustomed to travel a good deal, spoke of the qualities of the sort of men he employed, remarking on the superior, persevering energy of the English workman, whose untiring savage industry surpasses that of every country I have visited, Belgium, Germany and Switzerland not excepted'.

Many town-dwellers, toiling six days a week at their desk or workbench, would have reached breaking point, had not relative redistribution of wealth been matched by increased opportunities for recreation.

Thomas Cook, a Baptist missionary, conceived the idea of inexpensive organized tours and in 1845 ran a conducted excursion from Liverpool, charging 14 shillings each (70p) for first class pas-

Impression of Mendelssohn. Drawn by Aubrey Beardsley for the *Savoy* magazine, 1896.

sengers and 10 shillings each (50p) for second. The train left at five in the morning, each passenger being provided with a guidebook detailing places of interest. Bradshaw's *Railway Guide* was first published in 1841.

The excursion became quickly a social phenomenon. Seaside, countryside, dales, moorlands and fells were explored with an enthusiasm of which Mendelssohn would have approved. A certain James Payne hit the nail, somewhat aggrievedly on the head:

Our inns are filled to bursting, our private houses broken into by parties desperate for lodgings. A great steam monster ploughs up our lake and disgorges multitudes upon the pier; the excursion trains bring thousands of curious, vulgar people, who mistake us for the authoress next door [Harriet Martineau, a political writer who had taken Wordsworth's advice and built herself a rural retreat in Westmorland] and compel us to forge her autograph; the donkeys in our street increase and multiply a hundredfold, tottering under the weight of enormous females visiting our waterfalls from noon to eve; we are ruthlessly eyed by painters and brought into foregrounds and backgrounds as 'warm tints' or 'bits of repose'; our hills are darkened by swarms of tourists; our lawns are picknicked upon by twenty at a time, and our trees branded with initial letters.

Victorian art was as wide and varied as its social life. Favourite was Sir Edwin Landseer, who sculpted the lions in Trafalgar Square and painted stags at bay. There was the visionary genius of Turner, the lush romanticism of Constable.

Among writers and poets there was a dazzle of talents — Tennyson,* The Brownings, Carlyle, Macauley, Disraeli, Ruskin, Thackeray. 1847, the year of Mendelssohn's death, saw the publication of Charlotte Bronte's *Jane Eyre* and Emily Bronte's *Wuthering Heights*.

In the years when Felix was chasing across Europe, Charles Dickens was applying himself with equal zeal to the creation of a long series of masterpieces — *The Pickwick Papers, Oliver Twist, Nicholas Nickelby, Old Curiosity Shop, A Christmas Carol,* and *Martin Chuzzlewit*.

These were the books that made Dickens, three years Mendelssohn's junior, the most popular writer in England. In 1844 the two met. Mendelssohn, according to Dickens' daughter, quickly became the writer's favourite composer.

The Victorian age was, above all, one of optimism and activity, when the problems of the moment and their practical solution were the staff of life.

A census conducted on Sunday, 30 March, 1851 might well prove that out of 17,927,600 people able to attend church, the high proportion of 7,333,564 did so. Victorian society was, largely, a pious one. Obeisance had duly to be done, but life after death was, the church declared, assured. What mattered was the here and now. Macaulay spoke for an age when he surmised that 'an acre in Middlesex' was 'better than a principality in Utopia'.

---

* Tennyson once described Mendelssohn's as 'the most perfect face I have ever seen'.

120

It is hardly surprising that Mendelssohn and his music went down as well as they did. English audiences found in his music, gaiety, sentiment and charm. It was music without 'problems'. As for Mendelssohn the man, he conformed closely to the Victorian notion of ideal gentleman.

From the start, the press liked him and it is to his credit that he never attempted to curry favour. A measure of the critical regard he garnered, can be gained even from a silly review taken from *The Literary Gazette* [*sic.*] of June 6, 1829:

A German gentleman — with a long Christian name, too long for any Christian to pronounce with impunity — made his début on this occasion, and performed on the piano a piece termed on the card a 'concert-stück.' The pianist, however, never once *stuck* in his performance; but on the contrary appeared to get through his work with no less satisfaction to his audience than to himself.

The English loved Felix as much as they admired him. He was offered (but declined) the chair of music at Edinburgh University, and directorship of the Philharmonic Society. As Klingemann wrote to Rebecka, 'We, the John Bulls that we are, are more naive and more sincere than the people of the Continent, we possess the organ of veneration and admire willingly and honestly'.

Admiration extended as far as the Queen.

Felix first met Queen Victoria in 1842. Only five years a Queen, Victoria was still barely more than a girl and married ecstatically to 'that beautiful man', Prince Albert. Albert, whose gifts were more considerable than he is given credit for, regarded music as compensation for debarment as reigning co-Sovereign. It took time and diplomacy before even Victoria managed to obtain for her husband, a German and an outsider, a post as adviser and helper to the throne.

Albert, fed up and lonely for his homeland, spent hours at a time sitting forlornly at the organ. Lady Lyttleton, one of the Queen's attendants, once caught a glimpse of Albert's face as he played, seeing something 'which made her feel that only the instrument really knew what was in his soul'. Endowed with a fine tenor voice, he loved to sing duets with the Queen.

Victoria, too, enjoyed music,* and her journal contains a number of entries:

Mozart: *The Magic Flute:* Covent Garden, 1852
The opera itself was performed in a slovenly manner. The three lady attendants (on the Queen of the Night) sang very badly, the scenery was very inferior, and Mario really walked through his part (Tamino).

---

* Before her accession, she had taken lessons from the celebrated bass, Luigi Lablache. Famous for his breath control, Lablache once 'sang a long note from *piano* to *forte* and back to *piano;* then drank a glass without having breathed; then sang a chromatic scale up the octave, in trills, still in the same breath; and finally blew out a candle with his mouth open'.

It was to Albert, that Mendelssohn owed his invitation to Buckingham Palace. King Friedrich Wilhelm IV had furnished him
with a letter of introduction, Mendelssohn called and, on a second
visit, met the Queen for the first time.

As Elizabeth Longford has pointed out, the Queen in her younger
days was not insensitive to handsome men, 'frequently
(emphasising) her admiration for male beauty, often discussing the
handsome figure of one or other of her courtiers'. Not surprisingly,
she took to Felix.

Enjoying his rôle as royal dilettante, he wrote his mother a voluminous account of the meeting:

Prince Albert invited me for Saturday at half-past two, in order for me to try the
organ before I was to depart. I found him quite alone, and just as we were in the
midst of a conversation, in came the Queen, also quite alone and dressed in a
housedress. She said that she had to leave for Clermont in an hour. 'My God,
what a mess there is here!' she exclaimed, noticing that the wind had scattered
single sheets of a large, unbound score which was lying on the organ and blown
them into all corners of the room. So saying, she knelt down and began gathering
the sheets. Prince Albert helped, and I deigned to do likewise. The Prince
explained the various registers to me, and she said: never mind, she would
straighten the room up all by herself. Then I asked the Prince to play something
for me so that I could boast about that in Germany. He played a Chorale by heart,
pedalling nicely, cleanly, and without mistakes, so well that many a professional

Prince Consort and
composer alternate in
entertaining the young
Queen Victoria at the
keyboard. After a painting
by Carl Rohling.

organist could have taken it as an example. The Queen, who had finished her
work, sat down and listened with pleasure. Now it was my turn to play, and I
began my chorus *Wie lieblich sind die Boten* from *St. Paul.* Even before I had finished the first verse, both of them began to sing along. While I played, Prince
Albert manipulated the registers skilfully: first a flute, then at the forte at the C
major passage everything full, then an excellent diminuendo, and so on until the
end of the piece, and everything by heart. I was enchanted and happy.

The Prince of Gotha came along, and we conversed back and forth. The Queen
asked if I had composed any new songs. She loved to sing those which had already
been published. 'You must sing for him', said Prince Albert. At first she let
herself be coaxed a little. Then she felt that she could try her luck with *Spring
Song* in B major. 'That is, if it is still here for all the music has been packed away
for Clermont'. Prince Albert went to look for it but returned: 'It's packed up'. I
said 'Well, perhaps we can unpack it again'. She answered, 'We have to send for
Lady N.N. (I didn't catch the name.) She rang the bell, the servants ran in and
came back quite embarrassed. Whereupon the Queen went herself. During her
absence, Prince Albert said to me, 'She asks you to receive this gift as a momento',
and handed me a little case which contained a beautiful ring engraved with 'V.R.
1842'. The Queen appeared again and said, 'Lady N.N. has gone off and taken all
my things with her. I find that improper to the highest degree'. (You can imagine
how that amused me.) Now I said that she ought not to punish me by this little

* From a note dated St. George's Hall, 1859, the Queen evidently was not as
smitten as Felix with large-scale Bach. She wrote of the *St. Matthew Passion* that
'though so fine, it is a little fatiguing to listen to, there being so much sameness'.

mishap; rather she ought to choose something else to sing. After she had consulted her husband several times, he said, 'She will sing you something by Gluck'. In the meantime the Princess of Gotha joined us and so all five of us ambled through the corridors and rooms to the salon of the Queen, where beside the piano stood an enormous fat hobby horse and two big bird cages. The Duchess of Kent joined the party and while they all talked I browsed among the music papers and found my first 'Song Collection'. Of course I asked that she choose one of these songs rather than the Gluck. She agreed willingly, and what did she choose? *Italien.* [a song not by Felix, but Fanny]. She sang it most charmingly, strictly in tempo and cleanly in diction; only after the words 'der Prosa Last und Muh', when the melody goes to D and then rises harmonically, she sang twice a D sharp; then because both times I suggested the D on the piano she sang D at the third verse where D sharp is written. But apart from that little error, it was really enchanting, and the last long G I have never heard better, cleaner, and more naturally sung by an amateur. Now I had to confess that Fanny was the composer of the song. (This was hard, but pride goeth before a fall.) I asked her to sing one of the songs that were really mine. 'If you would do it, I'd do it gladly', she said, and sang, *Lass dich nur nichts dauern* without a single mistake and with truly felt expression. I thought it was not the occasion to indulge in extravagent compliments and therefore I merely thanked her several times. But when she said, 'Oh! if I hadn't been so nervous — usually I have a pretty long breath', then I praised her with a good conscience.*

Then Prince Albert sang, *Er ist ein Schnitter, der heisst Tod.* Then he said I had to play before I left. He gave me as the two themes for improvising the Chorale which he had usually played just before and the 'Schnitter' song. If proceedings had gone as they usually do when I really want to improvise well, I would have played horribly. Yes that happens to me frequently — and then I remember nothing but my anger. Yet this time, as if the gift I should receive were to be an unclouded memory, I played exceedingly well; I was in the vein, played for a long time, and I even enjoyed it. You can imagine that in addition to the two themes I also used the two songs which the Queen had sung. But I wove them in so naturally that I could have continued for ever. Both of them followed me with an understanding and an attention which put me into a better humour than usual when I improvise for an audience.

I forgot to say that I asked permission [granted] to dedicate the A minor symphony [*The Scottish*] to the Queen. This symphony was the real reason for my journey ... also that just as the Queen was about to sing, she said, 'Out with the parrot! He screams louder than I can sing'. Whereupon Prince Albert rang the bell and the Prince of Gotha said, 'I will carry him out myself'. And I said, 'Please permit me to do it'. And I took the big cage and handed it over to the astonished servants.

Victoria's journal entries confirm Felix's letters home:

June 16, 1842 ... After dinner came Mendelssohn Bartholdy, whose acquaintance I was so anxious to make. Albert had already seen him the other morning. He is short, dark, and Jewish looking — delicate — with a fine intellectual forehead. I should say he must be about 35 or 6. He is very pleasing & modest, & is greatly protected by the King of Prussia. He played first of all some of his *Leider ohne Worte* after which, his *Serenade* & then, he asked us to give him a theme, upon which he could improvise. We gave him 2, *Rule Britannia,* & the Austrian National Anthem. He began immediately, & really I have never heard anything so

Buckingham Palace, 1842. (Mansell).

---

* In old age, the Queen was sometimes heard to make the proud, but exaggerated, claim that Mendelssohn had been her teacher.

beautiful; the way in which he blended them both together & changed over from one to the other, was quite wonderful as well as the exquisite harmony & feeling he puts into the variations, & the powerful rich chords, & modulations, which reminded one of all his beautiful compositions. At one moment he played the Austrian Anthem with the right hand he played *Rule Britannia,* as the bass, with his left! He made some further improvisations on well known themes and songs. We were all filled with the greatest admiration. Poor Mendelssohn was quite exhausted, when he had done playing.

July 9 ... Mendelssohn came to take leave of Albert, previous to his returning to Germany, & he was good enough to play for us, on Albert's organ, which he did beautifully. As he wished to hear me sing, we took him over to our large room, where, with some trepidation, I sang, accompanied by him, 1st: a song which I thought was his composition, but which he said was his sister's, & then one of his beautiful ones, after which he played to us a little. We thanked him very much, & I gave him a handsome ring as a remembrance.

A few days were then spent with the Beneckes, cousins of Cécile's, at Denmark Hill in Surrey. One morning, when everyone else had gone for the day to Windsor, Felix sat down and wrote a further *Song without Words,* Op 62, No 6, the popular *Spring Song.*

Two years later, Felix was again in London, writing home that his season was as 'crazy' as anything he had experienced. He never managed to get to bed before half-past one each morning, and in the space of two months made as much music as he had during the previous year.

Once more he was the Queen's guest. They played and sang together, chatted, and Mendelssohn invited her to one of his concerts.

In 1842, the Philharmonic Society had recorded a deficit of £300. In 1844, with Mendelssohn in town, they could add £400 to their reserve fund. On 27 May, 1844 he introduced Joachim, now thirteen, to London in the Beethoven violin Concerto. Felix at the same time accepted a commission to supervise a critical edition of Handel's *Israel in Egypt.* In the event it might not have been quite what the commissioning body, the English Handel Society, expected. At a time when conductors blew out eighteenth-century instrumentation with nineteenth-century brass parts, Felix provided unretouched Handel, taken directly from the autograph score and first editions.

Birmingham Town Hall. (Radio Times).

Only once did he experience disappointment. He thought that London ought, like Leipzig, to have the chance of hearing Schubert's greatest symphony. But the orchestra would, like their Viennese counterparts, have none of it, the string writing and horn chording in the finale again causing merriment. Felix lost his temper and the performance was cancelled (so angry was he that he refused to release his *Ruy Blas* overture which had been urgently requested).

He received also an invitation to take charge of a major music festival planned for Birmingham in 1846. He would have an entirely free hand, able to hire and fire as he chose. He declined, however, pleading he had too much already to do.

At the same time, he wanted to express his great love for England

Jenny Lind (1820-87) the 'Swedish Nightingale'.

so he resolved that Birmingham should have the work that would, he considered, be the apogee of his achievement. He offered them *Elijah*. The star would be Jenny Lind.

Jenny Lind, the 'Swedish nightingale' remains the most controversial singing star of her own, or any other, age. When Mendelssohn met her, she was twenty-four and had just made a sensational début in Berlin, a slight, stub-nosed girl, austerely dressed and without a trace of the temperamental *diva*. Chorley wrote that 'her apparition was indeed a godsend among the clumsy and exaggerated women who strode the stage, screaming as they strode'.

Yet it was just this simplicity that Jenny Lind's detractors said was manufactured. They said that she was instead a vain and egocentric woman, who hid behind a façade. Henry Pleasants writes:

There was always a smugness and primness about Jenny Lind, a readiness to judge and deplore and condemn, a constant dwelling upon her own virtue and high-mindedness. Her whole life was a series of pious, sanctimonious attitudes, relieved, when she chose to turn it on, by compelling charm. More astonishing than any of her vocal miracles is the plain fact that she could put these attitudes over.

Jenny Lind could, in short, be night and day, depending on who she was with. In 1845, after her *Gewandhaus* début (at which Mendelssohn conducted), a supper was given in her honour by the Brockhaus family. Fritz Brockhaus recalled:

After the concert, Fräulein Lind promised to come to our house. The evening became a meeting of all the artists. Mendelssohn's joy over Lind as an artist and as a noble woman was infectious; he was all enthusiasm.

We were at the Mendelssohns for lunch with Lind. One has to like this girl from the bottom of one's heart. She is such a fine and beautiful character. Yet she is not happy. I am convinced that she would exchange all her triumphs for domestic happiness.

Josefa Durk-Kaulbach, daughter of the painter Wilhelm von Kaulbach, wrote in different vein:

My father offered her the hospitality of our home. One day the huge carriage which had been specially built for her arrived at our garden-portal, packed high with trunks and boxes. At once the carriage destroyed our carefully cultivated flowers and ruined our neat garden paths.

My father flew into a temper: he had made himself a different image of the Swedish Nightingale. Jenny Lind was a charming woman but as moody and capricious as she was charming. The crisis came the evening she sang Annchen in *Der Freischütz*. During the performance she had the ill-luck to lose a shoe. That ruined her mood, the public noticed it. The expected success did not materialise. There was an enormous company invited to our house and everybody was dying to meet the famous singer. Who did not put in an appearance? Jenny Lind. She locked herself in her room and would not answer knocks or pleas.

Yet, as an artist, Jenny Lind was simple and supremely affecting, her voice possessing a 'virginal purity'. Grillparzer wrote that when he heard her, he could not think of time or space but heard instead 'a soul singing'. When she made her London début (in Meyerbeer's

125

Robert le Diable), the crush was so great that men were pushed over, women fainted, and dress suits torn to tatters.

Mendelssohn and the Queen were both there, the latter throwing at the artist's feet a wreath. In her diary the Queen noted:

It was all *piano*, and clear and sweet, and like the sighing of zephyr; yet all heard. Who would describe those long notes, drawn out till they quite melt away; that 'shake' which becomes softer and softer, and those very *piano* and flute-like notes, and those round flesh tones which are so youthful?

From then on, everything was Jenny Lind 'servants' caps, cigars, flies for trout fishing, meerschaum pipes, spectacles cases, and several Staffordshire pottery figures modelled in her image'.

Flaring often into tantrums, Lind earned Felix's admiration nonetheless as an artist. The soprano part in *Elijah* he created around Jenny's voice. She, for her part, seems to have fallen more than a little in love with Mendelssohn. Although, according to Joan Bulman, 'she clamped down on her feelings', their companionship was close and exhilarating. Small wonder that Cécile looked at Lind askance.

At first it seemed as if Jenny would sing in *Elijah* at its première. Bulman writes:

Mendelssohn wrote it at a time when they were in almost daily contact, when the sound of her voice was ringing in his ears. He had studied her voice minutely, knew the timbre of every note. Each had a quality of its own. Of them all he loved best the upper F sharp, and often spoke admiringly of her *'wunderbares Fis'*. It is for her that the F sharps ring out in the opening bars of 'Hear ye, Israel'.

The *Gewandhaus* concert had been a spectacular success. Ticket prices were raised, and free admission for Conservatory students cancelled. The students protested and sent to Mendelssohn a delegation led by Otto Goldschmidt, a forceful young man with red hair. He was later to become Jenny Lind's husband and accompanist.

Whenever she wanted help, Felix was on hand. Anxious about appearing in Vienna, she prevailed upon Felix to write introductory letters to two old friends, Baroness Ertmann and Aloys Fuchs. In both, he referred to Jenny as his 'cherished friend'.

During the 1846 Lower Rhenish Music Festival at Aachen, the two took journeys together down the Rhine. He gave her a manuscript album of his songs, along with his portrait painted by Magnus.

Yet, despite all this fondness and attention, the mutual admiration, and some happy times together, Jenny Lind did *not* sing that first performance of *Elijah* in Birmingham in 1846. Only after Mendelssohn's death, did she sing the part. She then mourned him as 'the only person who brought fulfilment to my spirit, and almost as soon as I found him I lost him again'.

Mendelssohn's two last visits to England, were devoted primarily to *Elijah*. Moscheles had been appointed Director of the 1846

Left:
Title page of piano score
of the oratorio *Elijah*.
(British Museum).

Right:
Facsimile of a page of
Elijah (manuscript vocal
score).

Birmingham Festival, and *Elijah* was its chief attraction. Many details had to settled, the text of the oratorio translated into English (a task overseen by Klingemann), the casting discussed. At one moment Felix would write to his collaborator, Schubring about some problem or other over the libretto ('May Elisha sing soprano? Or is this inadmissable, as in the same chapter he is described as bald?'), at another about the Festival manager, Joseph Moore, who was keen to have excluded from the orchestra players who, on a previous occasion, had shown themselves backward.

Though the soprano part was intended for Jenny, Mendelssohn refused to negotiate with her. As a friend, he did not like to do so, while he felt it 'highly unlikely that I could get anything like a definite answer from her'. The part was eventually assigned to a Madame Maria Caradori-Allan who seemed quite literally out of tune with what was required of her. She demanded Mendelssohn transpose her big aria 'Hear ye, Israel' down a tone. Pointing out that he could easily find another soprano, Felix flatly refused to do so.

Mendelssohn arrived in London on 18 August and plunged into ensemble rehearsals held at Moscheles' home, followed by orchestral rehearsals in Hanover Square Rooms.

On the 23rd, the whole cast, along with a posse of newsmen, travelled by a special 'festival train' to Birmingham. There, further rehearsals were held with full chorus. As usual, Mendelssohn worked deep into the night, correcting orchestral parts. With an orchestra of 125 and a chorus of 271 this was in itself a gigantic undertaking.

A letter from
Mendelssohn to W.
Bartholomew concerning
publication of *Elijah*.
Bartholemew translated
text of *Elijah* into English
for the Birmingham
performance.
(British Museum).

The result, on 26 August, 1846 was a triumph; as Moscheles
wrote to his wife, 'something quite amazing'. It was not the done
thing to applaud oratorio performances but, on this occasion, such
niceties went by the board, swept aside (in the words of *The Times)*
by a 'volley of plaudits, vociferous and deafening', from an audience of two thousand. Even Felix managed to put aside his usual
reserve:

No work of mine ever went so admirably at its first performance, nor was
received with such enthusiasm by both the musicians and the audience as this
oratorio. It was quite evident at the very first rehearsal in London that they
liked it, and liked singing and playing it; but I confess, I was far from antici-
pating that it would possess such vigour and attraction at the first performance. If
only you had been there! During the whole three hours and a half that it lasted,
the big hall with its two thousand people and the large orchestra were all so con-
centrated that not the slightest sound could be heard from the audience, and I was
able to sway at will the enormous mass of orchestra and choir and organ. No
fewer than four choruses and four arias were encored, and in the whole first movement
there was not a single mistake. Later there were several in the second half, but
even these were unimportant. A young English tenor [Charles Lockey] sang the
last aria so beautifully I was obliged to exercise great self-control in order not to be
affected, and to beat time steadily.

Impression of
Birmingham by
Mendelssohn.

The soprano, though, evidently did not measure up. To Livia
Frege, a Leipzig singer and friend, Felix wrote:

With so much light the shadows were not absent, and the worst was the soprano
part. It was all so pretty, so pleasing, so elegant, at the same time so flat, so heart-
less, so unintelligent, so soulless, that the music acquired a sort of amiable expression about which I could go mad even today when I think of it.

As for the score, dissatisfaction with it as usual soon crept over
Felix. Back in Leipzig he started revising it. 'What?', Moscheles
queried in astonishment, 'Are you trying to make that beautiful
work even more beautiful?'. Felix called his habit of tinkering, his
'dread disease'.

A second version was ready for performance the following year
by London's Sacred Harmonic Society.

The Society asked Mendelssohn to conduct and once again he
could not resist. Little can he have known that his journey across
the channel was to be his last. Amoeba-like, what was supposed to
be one performance turned into six, four in London (at Exeter
Hall), one in Manchester and one in Birmingham. Overcome with
emotion, George Eliot wrote that *Elijah* for her represented 'a kind
of sacrificial purification of Exeter Hall'. Victoria and Albert were
present at the second London performance on 23 April, Albert
writing in Felix's copy of the libretto:

To the Noble Artist who, surrounded by the Baal-worship of debased art, has
been able, by his genius and science, to preserve faithfully, like another Elijah, the
worship of true art, and once more to accustom our ear, amid the whirl of empty
frivolous sounds, to the pure tones of sympathetic feeling and legitimate harmony:
to the Great Master, who makes us conscious of the unity of his conception,

Mendelssohn conducting the oratorio *Elijah* in Birmingham Town Hall, 1846. From *The London Illustrated News*.

Title page of *Scottish Symphony*, dedicated to Queen Victoria 1842.

through the whole of his creation, from the soft whispering to the mighty raging of the elements.

Inscribed in grateful remembrance by Albert.

Victoria was present again at a Philharmonic Society concert. Active as ever, the day before the Birmingham *Elijah* Felix conducted his *Scottish* Symphony and the *A Midsummer Night's Dream* music, and appeared as soloist in Beethoven's G major Piano Concerto. 'I wanted to play especially well', he wrote, 'because two ladies were present whom I wished to please, the Queen and Jenny Lind'. Nor was this the end. He took part in a number of chamber performances, put in two appearances at Buckingham Palace, and gave two receptions at the Prussian ambassador's where he managed to bump into the Prime Minister, Mr Gladstone.

The Queen noted:

After a very early dinner, we went at $\frac{1}{4}$ to 7 with the Dss. of Sutherland & the Ladies & Gentlemen, to Exeter Hall, to hear Mendelssohn's new oratorio of *Elijah*, which is extremely fine. He conducted himself, & the whole went off very well. The choruses are all very fine, in particular the one 'Hear our cry oh Baal', — the concluding Chorus of the 1st part, & the concluding one to the 2nd. There is one very fine Motet 'Cast they burden', &c, also a recitative & chorus between Elijah and youth, which precedes the conclusion of the 1st part. Then the chorus descriptive of the fire coming down, & the Motet and Chorus 'Holy, Holy'. The recitatives might be shortened, but the whole is a splendid work. We talked to Mendelssohn between the different parts.

Went to a Philharmonic concert, one of the best I ever remember but nothing came up to Mendelssohn's playing of the beautiful (Beethoven) concerto. It was so full of feeling and soul, & his touch was wonderful. He played entirely by heart, which, when doing so with the orchestra must be most difficult. He is a wonderful genius & is deservedly an amazing favourite here.

We had the great treat of hearing Mendelssohn play, & he stayed an hour with us, playing some new compositions, with the indescribably beautiful touch of his. I also sang 3 of his songs.

On 8 May, 1847 Felix took his leave of Victoria and Albert. So tired he could hardly lift his arms, he started his homeward journey. Time was running out.

Chapter 10

Envoi

Man's soul — how like the water,
Man's fate — how like the wind!
    — GOETHE

Felix could never say no. Any moment he planned to close his score, lay down his baton, put away his travelling bag and take a long, empty sabbatical. All he wanted, he said, was to find a quiet spot where he could amble through the fields, be with Cécile, play with his children and get down in earnest to the tricky business of composition. At thirty-seven, he had been before the public for the best part of a generation.

Yet only occasionally did he take time off. To Fanny, on 29 September, 1846, he wrote uncharacteristically:

I must be lazy for a little bit longer. In fact I've been idling since the moment I was asked to go to Manchester for two concerts but declined and went to London instead, where my only business was a fish dinner at Lovegrove's in Blackwall. Then I stayed another four days at Ramsgate to drink in sea air and eat shrimps and enjoy myself. I then stayed a day at Ostend because I felt sleepy, and another with the Seydlitzes at Cologne because I was too tired. Then four more at Horchheim, where my uncle walked me round in the boiling sun for an hour and a half in the vineyards, and kept up such a pace I was on the point of telling him I couldn't keep up, but felt ashamed, and stopped my mouth by stuffing it with grapes. Then I stayed at Frankfurt because I was so weary, and ever since I've been back in Leipzig I've been resting.

There he did nothing all day long, he said, save 'vegetate, eat, take walks and sleep'.

Something, however, always cropped up. Like Li Po's traveller, Felix must have longed for 'when a breeze waves, bringing fair weather' and he could 'set a cloud for sails and cross the blue oceans'. But just before the Birmingham Festival of 1847, for example, he was ranging as far afield as Aachen, Cologne, Düsseldorf and Liège. As soon as the Festival was over, he hurried back to Leipzig to split a heavy conducting schedule at the *Gewandhaus* with Gade (it was one of these concerts that Ferdinand David premièred the Violin Concerto).

Telltale signs of pressure began, here and there, to make themselves felt. On 5 November, 1846 Felix conducted the première of Schumann's second Symphony. During the course of the evening he met with an unpleasant reminder that the Protestant composer who had just completed a setting of the Catholic *Lauda Sion* was, after all, a Jew. The overture to Rossini's *William Tell* had been programmed for the first half of the concert, but so delighted were the audience the piece had to be repeated. A hostile critic thought this a cheap trick to delay first hearing of the Schumann, and said so, crudely and ungraciously. Felix, used to brushing aside such snipes, this time merely withdrew in hurt silence, too weary to say or do anything.

For his own music he had, by the New Year of 1847, a number of ideas in mind. For the Philharmonic Society in London, he planned to write another symphony. There was to be a third oratorio, *Christus*, of which only a few fragments found their way onto paper. These he played to Victoria and Albert, the Queen noting in her diary that:

For some time he has been engaged in composing an Opera & an Oratorio, but has lost courage about them. The subject of his opera is a Rhine Legend & that for the Oratorio, a very beautiful one depicting Earth, Hell & Heaven, & he played one of the Choruses out of this to us, which was very fine.

There was vague talk of a cello concerto for Piatti, with whom he had played the Sonata in D, vaguer still of another piano Concerto.

Mendelssohn's study. From a water-colour by Felix Moscheles, painted a few days after the composer's death.

133

Felix was absorbed chiefly by ideas for his elusive opera, more especially one that would make a suitable vehicle for Jenny Lind. Initially, *The Tempest* again came to mind and Augustin Scribe went so far as to draft a libretto. This, Felix wisely rejected.

Emanuel Geibel, promising as a lyric poet but only an indifferent dramatist, then suggested the Lorelei legend. Felix was at first enthusiastic. Devrient helped Geibel with the libretto, but the venture thereafter quickly ran aground. As we have seen, on 1 May, 1847 the Queen could write simply that Felix had 'lost courage'. Only three numbers survive.

On 3 February, Mendelssohn's thirty-eighth birthday was celebrated with much merriment. Paganini was there and cheerful amateur theatricals found Joachim and Moscheles acting out an elaborate charade on the word 'Gewandhaus'.

Yet more than ever Felix would complain of tiredness and, ominously, recurrent headaches. Despite his irrepressible vigour, he looked — and gave in conversation the impression — of being far older than his years. His skin had a dull, greyish pallor, his eyes were heavy and his hair showed streaks of silver-grey. In London, the Klingemanns were especially worried. When, in May 1847, Felix embarked for home, Karl was sufficiently concerned to accompany his friend as far as Ostend. Thereafter, he travelled alone, his weariness increasing when, at a small German border town, a police official mistook him for a politically suspect Dr. Mendelssohn and he was subject to some hours delay.

View of Guttanen-Haslithal. After a water-colour by Mendelssohn.

134

Felix had been at home only a day or two when there fell the single greatest blow of his life. On 14 May, Fanny had been rehearsing for one of her Sunday concerts. Sitting at the piano, her hands suddenly fell from the keys, her whole body in the grip of a paralytic stroke. She was carried into the next room, but never regained consciousness. By eleven that evening she was dead.

When Felix received the news, he collapsed. When eventually he recovered, he could not stop crying. Fanny's death was an incalculable loss. Thereafter, Felix talked only occasionally about composition and then halfheartedly. In mid-sentence he would interrupt himself, listlessly saying, 'What's the use? I'll not be here'. He wrote of Fanny:

What we have lost, and I above all — that we are not yet able to measure. With her kindness and love she was part of me every moment of my life. There was no joy I experienced without thinking of the joy she would feel with me. The wealth of this sisterly love spoiled me and made me proud. I half believe the tragic news will suddenly prove false. Yet I know very well it is all true. I will never, never be able to get used to it. Perhaps she is lucky, in her marvellously harmonious existence, not to have experienced the pain of old age, of life gradually ebbing — but for us it is hard. I have not been able to think about music; when I try to do so, everything in me seems desolate and empty.

View of Lucerne. After a water-colour by Mendelssohn.

Cécile thought it wise to take Felix on vacation, but a trip to Baden was not a success. They were there joined by Fanny's husband and son and Paul and Albertine Mendelssohn before making their way to Switzerland. Staying mostly at Interlaken, Felix was happy to

Henry Fothergill Chorley (1808-72). Shown in later life. English music critic.

do a number of line drawings and watercolours, but worked at music only fitfully. Eventually the restless and unhappy String Quartet in F was completed. After this came two middle movements of an unfinished quartet, and a number of smaller works including one of his finest songs, the sombre *Nachtlied*.

Felix accepted a few callers, among them the author and traveller Johann Köhl and the English historian Grote, described by Jenny Lind as 'a nice old bust in a corner; you could go and dust him'.

H.F. Chorley met Felix and was shocked by his appearance. He talked about Rossini's *William Tell* and Donizetti's *The Daughter of the Regiment* and enquired aboud Verdi, but Chorley's last memory of him was:

> ... the sight of him turning down the road, to wind back to Interlaken alone; while we turned up to cross the Wengernalp to Grindelwald. I thought even then, as I followed his figure, looking none the younger for the loose dark coat and the wide brimmed straw hat bound with black crape, which he wore, that he was too much depressed and worn, and walked too heavily.

For much of the time, he did not have the heart even to approach a piano. He was more inclined to improvise, in desultory fashion, on the organ of the little church at Ringgenberg on the Lake of Brientz. He also developed the habit of going for long walks on his own. It was, he said, the only way he could find any kind of peace.

In September, the family returned to Leipzig. Felix was scheduled to conduct in Berlin the first German performance of *Elijah,* thence to travel to Vienna, but as soon as he reached Berlin and was shown Fanny's room — untouched since her death, with *The First Walpurgis Night* still open at the piano — he broke down, and cancelled all further engagements.

Felix, it seemed, could no longer face the public. Back in Leipzig, one friend noted that he was 'much changed in looks... (he) often sat dull and listless without moving a finger'. Toward the beginning of October, he went for a walk with Ignaz and Charlotte Moscheles. Asked how he felt, he replied 'grey upon grey'. When Ignaz heard him play through his new string quartet at the piano, he confessed that he heard in it 'a deeply agitated state of mind'.

The end was nearer than anyone can have expected. That same evening, Felix went to a small house party at the home of Livia Frege. At one point, she left the room in order to fetch more lamps. When she returned, Felix was sitting on the couch, his hands cold and rigid. It was obvious that he had had some kind of seizure, but he refused the offer of a carriage home, saying he would prefer to walk himself warm. At home, Cécile found him again with cold hands. The following day, he suffered a shattering headache. The doctor was summoned, said it was nothing, and applied leeches.

After a little time in bed, Felix seemed to recover. Paul wrote that in the meantime that if need be he was ready to bring 'the entire medical faculty of Berlin' to Leipzig by special train. Yet despite an improvement and even a resumption of walks, Felix remained subdued. On 25 October, in what was to be his last letter, he wrote to

Paul, 'God be praised, I'm daily getting better, and my strength is returning', but adding more gloomily that 'I feel as if somebody were laying in wait for me, saying 'Stop! No more!''.

On 15 October, he had had a long conversation about the future of the Conservatory. On 28 October, he was with Cécile. He had taken his morning walk and was eating his lunch with a good appetite when a sudden paroxysm occurred, he began to talk in great excitement in English and then lost consciousness. The doctor came, and was again at a loss.

Two days later, Paul arrived from Berlin, Felix, by now confined to bed, spoke to him but was clearly far from normal and became excitable and agitated. Toward two in the afternoon of 30 October, Cécile beckoned Paul to her room. She was, he recalled, trembling and hardly able to control Felix. Having gently been scolded for making such a nuisance of himself, Felix smiled. Then, without warning, he uttered a piercing scream that distorted his entire face.

The following day the pains had subsided, but his face was that of a dying man. Cécile would not leave the room. When the family at last persuaded her to take an hour's rest, Felix's moaning could be heard through the entire house. He then started singing at the top of his voice, before slipping once more into unconsciousness. Fitfully he recognised those around him, but could only mumble into his pillow that he was 'Tired, so very tired'.

On the fourth of November, everyone knew he was beyond recovery. At a few moments before nine-thirty that evening he died, peacefully, in his sleep. Cécile said simply, 'Life lasts so long — how shall I live it alone?'.

Felix Mendelssohn. The last hours.

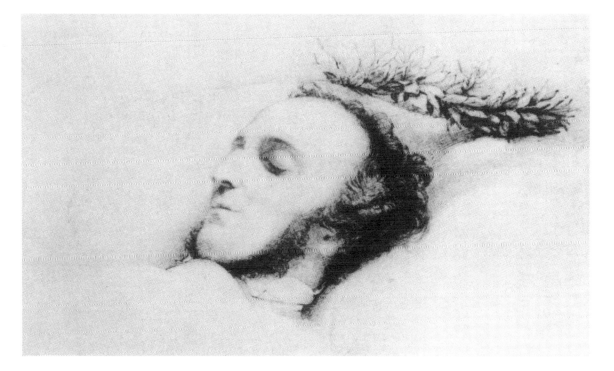

No final diagnosis of the cause of Felix's death exists. Klinge-mann said that he died from a series of strokes, adding that 'the dissolution had begun years before, of which severe nosebleeds, vertigo, headaches and irritability which often changed his whole temperament, were symptoms'. In all probability a brain artery ruptured.

A death mask was cast. Hensel and Eduard Bendemann both came and made drawings. A mob besieged the house, clamouring around the coffin and weeping. If Cécile or Felix's family and friends wanted to view him, the doors had firmly to be closed. Lit by torches, the room was heaped with flowers and wreaths. Cécile took a bunch of flowers and five little bouquets for the children and placed them over his hands, murmuring 'Who would believe it?'.

With Felix's death, the fountainhead ran thin though never dried completely. Four of Felix's children survived infancy (the last born, Felix, died when he was nine). The eldest, Karl, became a professor at Heidelberg. The second, Paul, was a gifted scientist who, like his father, died at the early age of thirty-eight. Of Felix's two daughters, the elder, Marie, married Victor Benecke; their son became a Fellow of Magdalen College, Oxford. Lili, who died at sixty-five, married Adolph Wach; a sympathetic picture of her is to be found in Ethel Smyth's *Impressions that Remained*.

Felix's sister, Rebecka, died of a stroke in 1858 at the age of forty-

Medallion of
Mendelssohn, modelled
by Knauer of Leipzig after
the composer's death, and
presented by him to the
Directors of the
Gewandhaus.

five. Paul lived to the age of sixty-two — longer by far than the others — having been a most devoted guardian to his nephews and nieces. Cécile lived for some time in Berlin. She then went to Baden, finally returning to Frankfurt and her own family. For a year before she died, she was so ill she had to be carried up and down stairs. Sad and withdrawn but, to the end, radiantly beautiful she died on 25 September, 1853.

The various branches of the Mendelssohn family became more numerous and ever more wealthy. Uncle Joseph's son, Alexander, saw Germany united under Bismarck and, in turn, his son, Franz, ennobled. Franz had two sons, Robert and Franz junior, the latter rising to become president of the German Chamber of Commerce. Ernst von Mendelssohn-Bartholdy, Paul's third son, added greatly to the wealth of the family banking house. When he died, in 1909, he was reckoned to be the wealthiest man in Berlin. A great-nephew of Felix, Arnold Mendelssohn, was an indifferent composer but a teacher of Hindemith. At the time of writing, Dr Karl Mendelssohn, a physicist and Fellow of the British Royal Society, has advanced important theories on the building of the pyramids. A great-grandson, Felix Gilbert, was in 1972 a professor of history at the Institute for Advanced Study of Princeton. George H. de Mendelssohn-Bartholdy is president of Vox Productions, New York.

In 1939, beaten about by the calamity of fascism, the Mendelssohn banking house was forcibly liquidated, and the few Mendelssohns still living in Germany dispersed, like seed before the storm, to the four corners of the earth. Some went to America, some to England, some to Switzerland, others vanished into oblivion. Like the twenty china monkeys, the family was broken up.

Three years earlier, Leipzig's monument to its composer had met a similar fate. Completed in 1892, Erwin Stein's statue of Mendelssohn dominated the square in front of the *Gewandhaus*. With the rise of Hitler, a campaign to have the monument removed gathered strength. As the *Leipziger Tagezeitung* fulminated on 16 September, 1936:

Without wishing to detract from the merits of the composer, it is undeniable that it goes against the healthy instinct of our nation when — prompted by false piety and consideration — we let stand a monument to a Jew, while we consistently endeavour to expunge the damage done to our cultural heritage by Judaism.

That 'damage' had been elaborated a few months earlier, in the course of an essay *Mendelssohn, Mahler and We* by Richard Litterscheid, in the March 1936 issue of *Die Musik*. Grudgingly admitting that *A Midsummer Night's Dream* 'is manufactured with almost unbelievable skill':

... it remains without true creative force proving that a Jew is not, and can never be, creative, not at least like a German genius.

Another Nazi verdict comes from a certain Karl Grunsky, writing in the *Westdeutscher Beobachter* for 3 March, 1935:

139

Mendelssohn's memorial in Leipzig. Demolished in 1936 as unacceptable to the ethos of the Third Reich.

Mendelssohn was an *Ersatz* for German masters. We no longer have any need for such substitutes, either in the concert hall, or in the home, or in church. Mendelssohn can perhaps still be used as material for practising, but never as a full-valued work of art. This holds true for the oratorios *St. Paul* and *Elijah* as well as the rest of his church music; Mendelssohn furnished easy *Ersatz* and through his own products hindered the acceptance of Bach, in which he himself was active. There is no excuse for the exaggerated value which the musical world has assigned to Mendelssohn in all branches.

A now-forgotten German musician even composed an *Ersatz* for the *Wedding March*.

It was only a matter of time before the government in Berlin issued orders to remove the 'monument standing before the *Gewandhaus* of the hundred-per cent Jew Mendelssohn-Bartholdie [*sic.*], because it creates public resentment!

To his credit, the Mayor of Leipzig, Carl Goerdeler (executed, in 1945, for his part in the plot the previous year to kill Hitler) protested. Such a move would, he said, do irreparable damage to Leipzig's reputation as a musical city. After all, was not Sir Thomas Beecham due soon to visit Leipzig with the London Philharmonic Orchestra as part of a continental tour?

Upon arriving, Sir Thomas duly enquired whether a delegation from the orchestra might place a wreath at the foot of the statue. Goerdeler replied that this would be a great honour. Unfortunately, he was out of town on the night of the concert.

In the morning, Sir Thomas and his delegation made their way to the *Gewandhaus*. But no statue was to be found. They looked everywhere; at the back, on the right, on the left side. What had happened? During the night (10 November, 1936) acting Mayor Haake, a Nazi bigwig, had commandeered a group of workmen and had the statue removed to a cellar. There it was hacked to pieces. The German press maintained a stiff silence. Thus did a once noble nation do honour to a composer who had given added lustre to its name.

*　　　*　　　*

Time, with its erasing hand, moves on. Phoenix-like, the Mendelssohn bank has risen recently from the ashes. In the woody Dahlem district of Berlin, there is, in George R. Marek's words, 'a concentration of wealth, fortunately housed' — the new University, the Dahlem Museum, the impressive new ethnological Museum, the Prussian State Library and the Jesuschristuskirche, where Pastor Niemoller preached his sermons against the Nazis, and famous today as a recording studio: all are there.

Adjacent to the music division of the Library, there stands a small building. This is the Mendelssohn Archive, devoted entirely to the Mendelssohns, Moses, Abraham, Felix and Fanny. The whole place is packed to overflowing with memorabilia, manuscripts, letters, Felix's toilet kit that he used when travelling, a silver goblet presented to his parents as a silver wedding anniversary gift.

Here, under the head of the Prussian State Library, his letters are being examined and collated, musical texts are being put under the microscope and meticulously corrected.

A visitors' book lies on the table. People come from all over the world, but the museum is still a quiet place. Looking at the portraits, surveying the manuscripts, weighing Mendelssohn's achievement in the balance, it is impossible not to reflect on the fragility of life and the transience of human endeavour.

At the same time, one can reflect that justice has handsomely been done; and that for Germany, Mendelssohn's music is once more considered a national treasure, luminous, alive, and infinitely precious.

London, 1978/9

Index

Illustrations are indicated in bold type

2/94 (17257)